Why Do They Dress That Way?

Stephen Scott

People's Place Book No. 7

Intercourse, PA 17534

Photograph Credits

Cover credits: front—Toyofumi Mor; back—Peter Zimberg

Perry Cragg: 5; William Lyons: 7, 77 top; John W. Bennet: 8, 72, 77 bottom, 106, 147; Fred J. Wilson: 11, 90, 93, 105, 115; Mel Liechty: 12, 88; Peter Zimberg: 15, 16, 59, 61, 83, 87 all, 116, 151; Mennonite Historical Library: 19, 21 both, 22 right; Quaker Biographies: 22 left, 110 both; Stillwater Friends Museum: 25; Lancaster County Historical Society: 27 left; Lancaster Mennonite Historical Society: 27 right; *Christian Living:* 29, 80 left, Beth Oberholtzer: 33 all, 37, 41, 100, 109 right, 155; Kenneth Pellman: 36 right, 67; Hunsberger Photography: 36 left, 94 left, 95, 103, 108, 109 left; *Hutchinson News:* 39; Joanne Siegrist Collection: 42 both; Lancaster Mennonite High School: 45, 47, 49; Kenneth Morse Collection: 53; Canterbury Shaker Community: 54; People's Bible College: 55; *The Catholic Witness:* 56; Irving Herzberg: 57; Peter Michael: 63, 111, 145; Richard Reinhold: 64, 75; Jeff Sprang: 71, 101; Clarence Hiebert: 74 top, 99; George Reimer: 74 bottom, 112 left; Stephen Scott: 79 both, 91; Frances Woodruff: 80 right, 96; *Family Almanac* (Mennonite): 85; *Louisville Courier Journal:* 89; F. W. Butterlin: 94 right; Gene Puskar: 102, 107; Ed Spiteri, Public Archives Canada, PA 131088: 112 right; Tom O'Reilly: 143.

Design by Dawn J. Ranck
Drawings by Stephen Scott

WHY DO THEY DRESS THAT WAY?

First published in 1986 (ISBN: 0-934672-18-0)
REVISED EDITION, 1997.
International Standard Book Number: 1-56148-240-4
Library of Congress Catalog Card Number: 86-81058

Library of Congress Cataloging-in-Publication Data
Scott, Stephen.
Why do they dress that way?
(People's Place Book; no. 7)
Bibliography: p.
Includes index.
1. Plain People—Costume. 2. Clothing and dress—Religious aspects—Christianity. I. Title. II. Series.
BX4950.S35 1986 248-4'6'088287 86-81058

Table of Contents

1.
Dress Is a Language

Dress speaks. One's clothing indicates one's identity and image, whether rock musician or sophisticated businessperson. Dress often makes a statement about an individual's social and economic status. Dress can communicate one's occupation: policeman, soldier, nurse, fast-food worker.

For special occasions many people proclaim their ethnic identity with festive costumes, be they Slavic or American Indian. Clothing expresses sacredness and hallowed tradition in religious ritual. It voices celebration and formality: the bride's gown, the orchestra conductor's white tie and tails . . .

One group of people's dress utters volumes about them though they are otherwise quiet and unobtrusive. They have adopted a kind of uniform but since they are never "off duty," most wear it constantly. They need no special festivities to reveal their identity and heritage. They wish to be reminded of it every day. They observe no sacred vestments in their worship; their clergy's appearance is little different from the layperson's. They have no special religious orders, but both men and women wear a religious garb. There are no formal dress or elaborate costumes used only for rare occasions. They avoid all ostentation and keep competition at a minimum by insisting on a uniform, simple dress.

Although diverse in background, these people—Amish, Mennonites, and Brethren—collectively are known as "plain people"—plain because they believe ornaments and finery are contrary to biblical principle.

The plain people's dress utters volumes about them though they are otherwise quiet and unobtrusive. (Amish—Ohio)

Plain Clothing Intentionally Separates

The plain people are Christians who believe discipleship encompasses every area of life, including dress. They do not separate doctrine from daily living. They are convinced that a true follower of Jesus Christ will be recognized not only by conduct and speech but also by appearance.

The plain people look different because they believe God's people should be distinctly separate from the surrounding world. The values and beliefs of a committed Christian are seen as radically opposed to those of the unconverted masses. They feel the world is controlled largely by Satan and the forces of evil. And so, they reason, conformity to the fads and fashions of popular society indicates identity with the world's system.

The plain people insist that the church, guided by the Word of God and not the dictates of fashion, should decide what a Christian should wear. They point out that the fashion centers have not been known for their righteousness. Economically, they judge the fashion industry to be a deceitful, greedy force. Keeping up with the latest styles is seen as wasteful, planned obsolescence.

Plain Clothing Purposely Identifies

To many plain people the most important value of distinctive dress is its usefulness in identifying the community of believers. Plain dress gives the wearer a sense of belonging and a feeling of kinship with brothers and sisters in the faith. Members of the same fellowship are immediately recognizable anywhere. One member of an Old Order group reflected that, "Seeing a fellow plain person when far from home is like hearing your own language spoken while traveling in a foreign land. There is an immediate bond of fellowship even though the person might be a total stranger."

The plain people take commitment to the brotherhood very seriously. An individual's dress is considered part of the united testimony of the group. Unbecoming conduct not only affects a member's own testimony and relationship with God, but the reputation of the whole church as well.

By wearing distinctive garb, plain people are constantly conscious of being outwardly identified as Christians and so,

The plain people look different because they believe God's people should be distinctly separate from the surrounding world. (Amish—Pennsylvania)

ideally, they seek to make their conduct consistent with their dress. A Mennonite woman told how as a girl her father decided to take the family to an amusement park. He thought this would be innocent fun even though such entertainment was frowned on by their church. While they were at the park, the father overheard someone say in a disgusted tone, "Mennonites—what are they doing here?" The family went home and never returned to such a place again.

Many plain people are not well versed in the scriptural and moral reasons for wearing plain clothes. They merely have faith that the church has preserved and upheld an appropriate standard of dress for Christians. Their clothing represents their identification with the body of believers and its total belief and value system. Many do not think of their dress as plain clothing or even Christian clothing, but as Amish clothing or Hutterite clothing, etc.

Nearly every plain church has arrived at some kind of standard to govern the dress of its members. Some rules are spelled out specifically while others are general and subject to individual interpretation. There is usually an understanding of what is

To many plain people the most important value of distinctive dress is its usefulness in identifying the community of believers. (Hutterites—Saskatchewan)

appropriate and what is not, even in the inexplicit areas. Some of the prescribed modes might not be of obvious religious significance. They are sacred not because of their intrinsic value, but because they have become symbols of identity for the group. These symbols include such things as tie strings on women's caps, peplums on the backs of dresses, and hooks and eyes on men's coats.

Compliance Indicates Commitment

To deviate from the standards and customs of the church is to declare one's dissatisfaction and lack of commitment. The transgression itself might be of minor significance but becomes an acid test to determine one's inward attitudes. Wearing that which is contrary to the order of the church is seen as evidence of a rebellious, worldly heart.

The value of being a separate people is not always obvious to those brought up in the plain way. Many have only learned to appreciate their distinctive dress after a period of questioning and doubt. Others never come to this conclusion.

A story in *Family Life* magazine, an Amish publication, tells how a girl, traveling far from home, became painfully ashamed and embarrassed by her black shawl and bonnet. She felt that everyone in the bus station was staring and whispering about her. Finally, in a moment of frustrated rebellion, she jerked off her shawl and stuffed it in a bag and hid her bonnet among her luggage.

In her new freedom, she browsed around the station without her old inhibitions. One of her first observations was a young man smoking a cigarette while gazing at a pornographic magazine. Later, while waiting on the bus, she observed a woman wearing excessive makeup who could hardly walk because of her tight clothes. She also remembered a bunch of boys who had whistled at her and made some suggestive remarks as she crossed the street. She concluded that these people were certainly not ashamed to be seen doing evil—why should she be ashamed to do good? She hurried off the bus before it departed and asked the driver to give her the bag containing her shawl.

Other plain people have told about being asked to watch the luggage of complete strangers in a train or bus station. Plain clothing has conveyed an image of religious devotion as well—some plain Christians have been approached by strangers asking for prayer. The plain people feel very unworthy of this kind of recognition and are especially saddened when any among their number do not live up to the expectations of others.

2.
The Religious Basis for Plain Clothing

Despite accusations to the contrary, plain people do not believe that clothing is the essence of Christianity. But while most would say that plain dress is not essential to salvation, they do agree that if they want to carry out the full will of God they will be separate from the world in their dress.

For most plain people, dress is a rather minor issue in their total belief system. But they do not take lightly the importance of nonconformed attire. Plain churches are convinced that modest, simple dress is essential to real Christian discipleship and must be maintained. Since the larger society places much importance on dress, the plain churches have also had to emphasize it and sometimes seem to have given this area disproportionate attention. They have used stern measures to counteract widespread and recurrent disobedience.

Why do the plain people continue to observe practices which have been disregarded by nearly all of Christendom and abandoned by most of the members in their own faith family? Those who wear plain clothing point to many biblical Scriptures to explain their practices: from the New Testament, ". . . straight is the gate and narrow is the way which leadeth unto life and few there be that find it."[1] And from the Old Testament they explain that it was only Noah and his family who escaped when the earth was destroyed the first time. Many plain people see the large-scale putting off of

Plain churches are convinced that modest, simple dress is essential to real Christian discipleship and must be maintained. (Swartzentruber Amish—Ohio)

The practice of wearing plain clothing is based on a number of scriptures and scriptural principles. (Amish—Indiana)

plain clothing as part of the apostasy of the end times, and refer to the biblical prophecy concerning "a great falling away."[2]

Nonconformity a Religious Principle

The plain people are convinced that nonconformity is a New Testament principle with direct implications for their clothing: "And be not conformed to this world but be ye transformed by the renewing of your mind,"[3] for example, and elsewhere, "As obedient children not fashioning yourselves according to the former lusts in your ignorance."[4]

Plain Christians regard the world as a hostile environment for the true believer. They do not expect to receive the approval of the larger society. Instead they remember Christ's words, "If ye were of the world, the world would love his own: but ye are not of the world, but I have chosen you out of the world, therefore the world hateth you."[5] They believe that Scripture cautions against the consequences of worldly enjoyment: "Love not the world, neither the things that are in the world. If any man love the world, the love of the Father is not in him. For all that is in the world, the lust of the flesh, and the lust of the eyes, and the pride of life, is not of the father but of the world. And the world passeth away and the lust thereof: but he that does the will of God abideth forever."[6]

So Christ's followers are seen to be distinctly separate from the world: "Wherefore come out from among them and be ye separate, saith the Lord."[7] And the people of God are referred to as "a peculiar people," "strangers," and "pilgrims."[8]

Humility Stressed

Humility is also a central theme for the plain people. Again, the teaching is rooted in Scripture: "Yea, all of you be subject one to another, and be clothed in humility: for God resisteth the proud and giveth grace to the humble."[9] These people's written statements of belief from the earliest times repeatedly warn against the evil of pride.

Once at a country sale a plain man and a fashionable man were discussing the relationship between plain clothing and humility. The fashionable man insisted there was no connection between the two. But when the plain man suggested they trade hats and walk around the sale grounds, the other man refused the offer.

Plain people believe strongly that Christians should all be on one social level. They consider displaying wealth through clothing an overt expression of pride. A uniform plain garb avoids this evil, they reason.

Not immune to temptation, the plain people realize that "pride in plainness" can develop. "The worst kind of pride is plain pride," they admit. There are individuals in nearly every plain community who go to great extremes to elevate their supposed humility, sometimes by sloppiness and uncleanliness. Such people are comparatively rare, however, and do not find favor in the churches. Plain people would agree, though, that the misapplication of a principle is not a legitimate argument for its abandonment.

Modesty Is Essential

Modesty is seen as an important Christian virtue which naturally accompanies humility. The necessity of adequate clothing appears in the very beginning of the Bible, where sin made Adam and Eve ashamed of their nakedness. It is stated that God did not approve of the scanty fig leaf aprons that the first humans hurriedly threw together, and so God replaced them with more ample coverings of animal skins. Sincere plain people wish to conceal the forms of their bodies, rather than reveal them. They refer to the New Testament story of the Gadarene madman who lived naked in the tombs. After Christ cast devils out of him, he was found "clothed and in his right mind."[10]

There is a story told of an older plain man riding in a car, who, when the vehicle came to a stop at a traffic light, looked out the window to see a scantily-clad young woman standing on the sidewalk. Seething in righteous indignation, the old man sputtered, "You're going to hell, and you're going to take a lot of men with you!" Most plain people discipline themselves to be quiet in their behavior and not given to such outbursts. The man's sentiments do, however, reflect the plain people's strong underlying feelings about modesty in dress.

Western society has become increasingly more permissive in the exposure of flesh. The plain people believe modesty requires more than being a little more covered than what is currently socially acceptable. Modesty should not be relative, they contend.

For example, a non-Amish family visited in the home of an Old Order Amish family. When the conversation turned to modesty, the visiting mother thanked the Amish man for bringing up the subject because she was concerned that her own daughter's dresses were too short. To demonstrate her own and her church's standard of decency, the woman knelt forward to show that her skirt touched the floor while kneeling. The Amish father couldn't bring himself to tell her that he considered this immodest also.

To avoid the difficulty of swimming suits, most plain churches prohibit mixed bathing of any kind. An occasional dip in a secluded spot by a group of the same sex is not forbidden, however.

Specific Teachings in the Bible

Two Scriptures in particular provide guidelines for plain people in matters of dress. One states, "In like manner also that women adorn themselves in modest apparel, with shamefacedness and sobriety; not with braided hair, or gold, or pearls, or costly array, but (which becometh women professing godliness) with good works."[11] Another is, ". . . let it not be that outward adorning of plaiting the hair, and of wearing of gold or of putting on of apparel, but let it be the hidden man of the heart, and quiet spirit, which is in the sight of God of great price."[12]

From such verses the plain people learn that their dress should be modest, simple, and economical, and that jewelry (including wedding rings) and elaborate hairdos are inappropriate for the Christian. By a lack of emphasis on external beauty, the plain people believe the inner virtue of the heart can better shine through. They also think that if one's mind is not preoccupied with beautifying one's body, a person can be free to do the Lord's work.

Cleanliness Is Valued

Most plain people firmly believe the maxim, "Cleanliness is next to godliness." They see slovenliness as disrespect for one's

"That women adorn themselves in modest apparel with shamefacedness and sobriety." (Old Order Mennonite—Ontario)

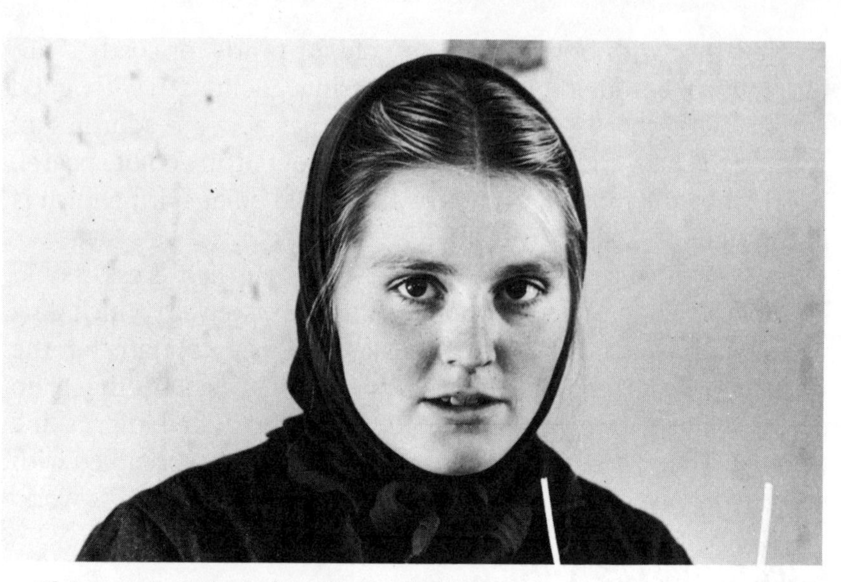

Plain people believe that simple clothing allows the inner virtue of the heart to shine through. (Amish—Ontario)

God-given body and a poor testimony to the world. It is true that most conservative Old Order people do not see the need for more than the traditional Saturday night bath. One person said she would rather smell some honest sweat than strong, artificial perfume.

Plain people do appreciate physical beauty. They admire pure, natural beauty and there are many examples among their members. It is the glamour that comes from a bottle that they regard as cheap, artificial, and tawdry. Cosmetics of all varieties and degrees (including leg-shaving in the more conservative circles) are seen as needless vanities. Outward attractiveness, not accompanied by a "meek and quiet spirit," is believed to be of little value, even harmful.

Additional Biblical References

On Pride:

Proverbs 16:18, *"Pride goeth before destruction, and a haughty spirit before a fall."*

Proverbs 6:16, 17, *"These six things doth the Lord hate: yea, seven are an abomination unto him: A proud look . . ."*

James 4:6, *". . . God resisteth the proud, but giveth grace unto the humble."*

On Worldliness:

Colossians 3:2, *"Set your affections on things above, not on things on the earth."*

James 1:27, *"Pure religion and undefiled before God and the Father is this, to visit the fatherless and widows in their affliction, and to keep himself unspotted from the world."*

James 4:4, *"Ye adulteresses, know ye not that friendship of the world is enmity with God? Whoever therefore will be a friend of the world is the enemy of God."*

On Nonconformity:

Zephaniah 1:8, *". . . I will punish the princes, and the king's children, and all such as are clothed with strange apparel." (This infers that there was a special type of clothing for God's people.)*

Numbers 15:38, 39, *"Speak unto the children of Israel, and bid them that they make them fringes in the borders of their garments throughout their generation, and that they put upon you a fringe, that ye may look upon it, and remember all the commandments of the Lord, and do them . . ." (The children of Israel wore a distinctive garb.)*

On Modesty:

Matthew 5:28, *"But I say unto you, that whosoever looketh on a woman to lust after her hath committed adultery with her already in his heart."*

Revelation 1:13, *". . . one like unto the Son of man, clothed with a garment down to the foot . . ." (A guideline for appropriate coverage.)*

Revelation 3:18, *" . . .that thou mayest be clothed and that the shame of thy nakedness do not appear . . ."*

3.
Where Did the Plain Pattern Come From?

What is the origin of the cut and pattern of plain clothing anyway? Did Christ wear a plain coat and the apostles dress in broadfall pants and suspenders? Did some mystic of old see a vision of how properly dressed Christians should look? Did an inspired believer sit down at his drawing board and design a style of clothing based on scriptural principles? None of the above seem to be the case.

Several scholars have theorized that plain dress is an adaptation of styles that were once fashionable or a carry-over from peasant clothing (also said to have a fashionable origin). It is often explained that the various plain groups merely latched onto certain items of apparel, not of their own design, and "froze" them into a static religious costume.[1]

It is also commonly stated that the early Anabaptists, the spiritual ancestors of the Mennonites, Amish, and Hutterites, prescribed no special garb for their followers. A distinctive cut of clothing is thought to have been a comparatively recent development. Some historians have stated that plain dress was instituted by the Mennonites in the late 19th century as a substitute for the separation that the German language had provided until that time.[2]

There is an element of truth in most of these suppositions, yet they do not give the full pictures and are, hence, misleading. They do not explain why certain types of clothing were accepted and others rejected.

How Did the First Plain People Dress?

The documentary evidence related to early Anabaptist dress is rather fragmentary but, taken as a whole, can lead to certain conclusions concerning the appearance of these first plain people. In Switzerland, from the very beginning of the Anabaptist movement in 1525 down to the mid-19th century, there are numerous references to the distinctive dress of these people.[3] In

An Anabaptist (probably Amish) farmer from an 1841 French farmer's almanac.

Holland, Menno Simons (from whom the Mennonites are named) had a great deal to say about pompous dress,[4] but several references in the *Martyrs Mirror* indicate that some Dutch Anabaptists could not be picked out in a crowd by their persecutors.[5] By the 18th century only a few groups of Dutch Mennonites practiced wearing distinctive garb.[6] (George Fox, founder of the Society of Friends [Quakers] preached simplicity in dress and his most zealous followers could be identified by their plainness in attire for over 250 years.)

Not much in the way of written rules and regulations on dress has been left behind by the early plain people. The earliest confessions of faith say little or nothing about clothing. Some historians have concluded this lack of written directives indicates that the church fathers placed little emphasis on dress. On the other hand, the early Anabaptists may have conveyed their order of dress orally or by example, as many very conservative groups of plain people do today. These contemporary plain people will leave behind little or nothing in print spelling out their dress practices. Often when a group's distinctive clothing (and other practices) are threatened do written rules first appear.

In many areas where the Anabaptists were found in 16th century Europe, sumptuary laws were imposed on the populace. Men of low estate were forbidden by law to indulge in ostentatious finery.[7] The aristocracy proudly reserved this privilege for themselves. If the Anabaptists dressed as peasants were decreed to dress, which would be in keeping with their emphasis on humility, they would have been very plain and simple. From historical documents it is obvious that the Anabaptists in Switzerland went beyond the legislated peasant simplicity.[8]

Differences Develop

Most sumptuary laws were either ignored or abandoned by the 18th century. While many peasants then exercised great freedom in adopting lavish costumes (although very standardized in each community), others, including the plain people, continued wearing very simple clothing.[9] These simple styles of the commoner were remarkably similar over a wide area and changed

Eighteenth Century Swiss Anabaptists.

very little over the years.[10] Often the "high church" Protestant neighbors of the plain people were nearly as simple in their dress as the plain people. But a more marked difference developed when these non-plain people began following the rapidly changing urban fashions.

When stylish, ready-made clothing became cheap and easily available in the 19th century, most country people gladly stepped aboard the constantly revolving fashion merry-go-round which heretofore was only accessible to wealthy riders.[11] The plain people saw danger in letting the whims of worldly fashion dictate what they as Christians should wear. Even though they could have afforded to do otherwise, they continued to observe the time-honored simple dress which had become a symbol of humility.

It was after the period of persecution and sumptuary laws that plain clothing began to develop into its present form. It took several hundred years for the various symbols of nonconformity to become fixed. Some of these symbols have a much longer history than others. Each item of plain dress became established by a very slow process of group consensus. For the most part,

(Left) Moses Brown (1738-1836), a Pennsylvania Quaker. (Right) Henry Brenneman (1791-1866), a Mennonite from Ohio.

every generation regarded the prayerful decisions of their forefathers as binding. Accommodation to current fashions was kept minimal. Selectivity and careful scrutiny were exercised. Practices were accepted or rejected within the context of an all-encompassing Christian belief system.

The plain people have sought to control cultural influences rather than be controlled by them. So what has resulted is their own kind of counterculture, rooted in Christian understanding. Their intent is to create a system for living, including dress, that is faithful to their beliefs and serves as an effective hedge against assimilation into the world.

Prerequisites for Plainness

It is apparent that many religious, social, and historical factors have helped to develop plain dress. By studying the history of the individual garments incorporated into the plain costume and considering the religious principles for which the plain people have historically stood, one can make certain observations and conclusions.

Identity with the Common Man

The plain people have always identified with common country folk. This is part of their emphasis on humility. Some of the items of plain dress, often attributed to a high fashion origin, can actually be traced to a peasant beginning. While women's bonnets became fashionable in the early 1800s there is ample evidence of their use among the peasantry in the late 18th century.[12] The large, shallow-crowned, flat hats worn by many plain women in the 18th and early 19th centuries were fashionably popular for a time, but their common name, "milkmaid hat," reveals their rural beginning.[13] Long trousers were also found among common folk long before they enjoyed fashionable acceptance. Many plain people probably adopted these items during their period of peasant use and continued wearing them after they became fashionable.

Clothing with a Purpose

The plain people have tried to choose attire consistent with their emphasis on simplicity and modesty. They feel strongly that clothing should be functional. Thus, a coat buttoning to the neck seemed more practical than one with useless lapels folded back only to reveal a ruffled shirt or fancy neck cloth. Long pants appeared more modest than knee breeches and the broadfall closing on trousers more modest than the fly front.[15] Of course the cape, apron, and long skirt served to conceal the feminine form, and the bonnet put into practice the "shamefacedness" spoken of in the Bible.

Even though the plain people derived some of their clothing from that of the simple country folk, they often simplified it further still. For example, the plain frock coat differs from the typical 18th century man's coat in that it has no outside pockets. The Amish use hooks and eyes rather than buttons on their coats and vests.

Fads and Fashions are Forbidden

It is evident from the writings of the first plain people that there was a strong conviction against worldly fashions. Since clothing should be durable and enduring, extreme temporary fads were forbidden. Early leaders, such as Menno Simons, made detailed lists of items they considered vain and foolish. As long as something was the latest fashion, it was considered inappropriate by those wishing to be nonconformed with the world. Some new styles of clothing did eventually gain acceptance; others were permanently forbidden.

The Good Old Way

Old-fashionedness has played an important part in the formation of plain clothing. The plain people have intentionally chosen to be behind the times in their appearance. Their refusal to follow every whim of fashion conveys an image of stability. Old-fashioned dress can also signify humility. Only the proud, these people reason, seek recognition by keeping in step with the latest styles.

Some items which came into the plain costume via the old-fashioned route may not meet some of the other criteria usually bearing on these people's choice of dress. In these instances the sanctity of being time-honored overruled apparent inconsistencies. For example, the "matz" headpiece of the Old Colony Mennonites could hardly be called simple.

While many elements of plain clothing can be traced to garments that were once worn by the general population, written and pictorial evidence indicates that these items were not worn by the plain people during their fashionable peak. And the plain people were slower to accept some items than others. Thus, their combination of clothing would never quite match those of the surrounding world. Today some plain women wear a 17th century style dress with an 18th century style bonnet and a 19th century century shawl.

It is evident that the plain people have been selective in the clothing items they have adopted. Plain dress does not represent the frozen ensemble of one particular era or area. The plain coat does resemble the 18th century man's coat, but that period's powdered wig, three-cornered hat, ruffled shirt, knee breeches, and shoe buckles did not become part of the plain dress.

Conservative Friends (Quakers) from eastern Ohio in the early 1900s.

The Propriety of Plainness

An important criterion for plain clothing is that it be characterized by a sense of propriety; so, the plain people have often adopted symbols shared by other groups wishing to demonstrate the same principles. The plain, wide-brimmed hat, for example, is also a religious symbol for some Catholic and Protestant religious orders and the uniforms of some nurses and charitable institutions.[16]

The similarity in dress among the various plain groups has often been explained as a matter of copying or borrowing. The Quakers are usually credited with originating plain dress (although some Quaker historians believe they got their dress from the Mennonites). There was no doubt some interdenominational borrowing, but this does not explain why some groups who were very isolated from each other appeared very similar in their dress: for example the Amish and the Shakers. It is more probable that the similarities indicate a widespread response and recognition of commonly known religious symbols.

A recent example of the development of such a symbol might serve to show how other symbols became established. In the late

19th century a style of man's haircut was introduced which featured short, tapered sides and back and side part. By the early 20th century this was the standard haircut in the Western world and remained so until mid-century. When the Beatles came along in the '60s with their mop tops, a new revolution in men's hair styles began. A few religious minorities refused to condone the shaggy look. They associated this style with the low morals and irreverence of the singing groups which introduced it. They also pointed to the biblical injunction against long hair on men. So such diverse groups as conservative Mennonites, Moonies, and Wesleyan Methodists made the short haircut a symbol of piety. These groups hardly copied one another. The new symbol was valid in that it was universally recognized even though it had a nonreligious origin.

Good Times and Immoral Times

Some periods of history have been known for higher morals than others which have the reputation of decadence. Many items of plain dress developed during or were selected from times of higher morals and religious respect. On the other hand, the fashions of morally-loose eras sometimes had a reactionary effect on the plain people. In these cases some of the styles of the preceding era were maintained in order not to be identified with the lower moral standards of the new period. This is especially true of women's dress.

This process extends back at least to the 17th century. The basic elements of the more conservative plain woman's costume are identical to those of the mid-1600s, the Puritan era. The unpretentious combination of cap, kerchief, apron, jacket bodice, and long skirt were distinctive to that prudent period.[17] This costume, which was never really high fashion, endured among the common classes for over two hundred years (which gives it additional favor with the plain people).[18]

The Puritan-based dress received new strength in the early 1800s as a reaction against the immodest dress and low morals of that decade. The German Baptist Brethren made a very strong statement against the new fashions in 1804, "Concerning the evil which grieves God and angels in heaven, and also faithful souls on earth, namely, the new fashions which are in vogue in the world . . . "[19] Even in New England a Congregationalist minister decried the flimsy Greek-inspired attire in 1811. "A young lady dressed *á la Grecque* in a New England winter violates alike good sense, correct taste, sound morals, and the duty of self preservation."[20] It was also during this time that the man's button-to-the-neck, standing-collar coat became established as a religious symbol in lieu of the relatively new coat with flaring lapels and turnover collar.[21]

While plain women could not identify with the flamboyant fashions of the 1820s and 1830s, they could look with favor on the styles of the 1840s which brought about a sense of respectability and sobriety in dress. The shawl and bonnet become symbols of these early years of Queen Victoria's reign and became fixed expressions of modesty and simplicity among many plain groups. While plain women did not adopt the voluminous crinolines and bulging bustles of the latter 19th century, they could accept the high-top shoes and black stockings of this era as aids to modesty.

The plain people were shocked into a new tenacity for their traditional dress by the unprecedented revealing fashions of the

Mary Brackbill Eshleman (1769-1848, left) and Anna Stauffer Hershey (1798-1875, right) were both Mennonites in Lancaster County, Pennsylvania.

1920s. During this time a number of fashions were introduced which even mainline Protestants and civil magistrates tried to curb. Hemlines rose to the knee for the first time, women's hair was cut short, makeup was used more extensively than ever before, stockings became sheer and flesh-colored, slacks and shorts became acceptable for some activities.

Most sociologists agree that this disintegration of traditional standards of decency was brought about by the impact of World War I.[22] To the plain people the world had never appeared more worldly. In the eyes of many plain people, morals have increasingly degenerated since that time. They do not wish to be identified with that trend and so have made a greater effort to separate themselves from the masses.

The revival of plain dress among Mennonites started in the 1880s and is said by some scholars to have been an effort to provide a means of separation from the world which the German language had provided before this time. It is often stated that uniform plain dress was not an issue until evangelists from the midwestern United States promoted it at the turn of the century. Numerous documentary evidences, however, indicate that American Mennonites were distinctive in their appearance from the early 18th century down to the 20th century.[23]

The extremely plain dress of the Reformed Mennonites, who separated from the main body in the late 18th century, was part of their effort to maintain true Mennonitism. The Stauffer Mennonites, an 1845 division from the Lancaster Mennonite Conference, kept a strong emphasis on both plain clothing and the German language, as did the various groups of Old Order Mennonites which formed from 1872 to 1900.[24]

It is true that by the late 19th century many Mennonites were no longer dressing plain and in some areas plain dress had never been very strong.[25] The promoters of plain dress saw uniformity in dress as the most effective means of combating worldly fashions. It was not a new idea. The Amish had taken this approach since their beginning in 1693.[26] To a lesser extent the Brethren,[27] River Brethren,[28] and Quakers[29] had the same emphasis. These three groups were well known to most Mennonites.

A Mennonite Sewing Circle near Harrisonburg, Virginia, 1948.

In the early 20th century, among the more conservative parts of the moderate majority groups of plain people (the Mennonite Church, the Church of the Brethren, and the Brethren in Christ Church), plain dress was modified in a number of ways. These included women eliminating aprons on their dresses and tie strings on their head coverings, and men substituting frock coats for sack coats and belts for suspenders.

While most individuals within the moderate groups today have replaced distinctive plain clothing in part or in whole with fashionable dress, the basic pattern preserved by those who still dress plain has remained basically the same as the conservative plain styles of the 1920s and '30s.

Very few new symbols of nonconformity have been introduced since then. The wide-brimmed hat, plain frock coat, broadfall pants, suspenders, and high shoes for men, and the cap head covering, bonnet, shawl, cape, apron, black stockings, and long dress for women have remained virtually the same for the last sixty years among Old Orders.

As a group moves away from plain dress toward fashionable dress, the pattern of change follows a very similar course, the main difference being the fashionable details added in the final stages prior to total abandonment of plainness.

Those wary of continuing change, however, make an on-going effort to halt its progress. The point of reference maintained by those groups is usually the dress patterns held before the moral decline of the 1920s.

How Symbols Have Changed

It appears that plain clothing has undergone changes through the years in at least two different ways. The one that causes the least friction is when an item of clothing that has not been established as a primary religious symbol or badge of group identity is replaced by another item that has become regarded as conservative or old-fashioned by the general population. In many plain groups shoes and eyeglasses are two items that have gone through this process of change.

Change happens also when symbolic plain clothing is replaced with stylish clothing or when symbols are modified to conform more closely to contemporary fashion. This process is regarded as "drift" by the plain people. This kind of change begins when one individual tests the established dress boundaries. If this person is successful in avoiding censure from the church authorities, then others will follow until eventually the whole group will accept, perhaps very reluctantly, a new style. When a group, community, or individual church makes such a change, others are often influenced to follow suit.

Plain groups may observe very different kinds of symbols, and those who do share the same symbols may place varying degrees of importance on them. For example, beards, as well as hooks and eyes, are important symbols to the Amish but are foreign to nearly all Mennonites. Old Order Amish males always wear broadfall trousers, but among Wenger Mennonites these are worn only by married men and then only for church (ministers wear them all the time). The polka-dot head scarf is a very distinctive symbol to Hutterites but is not shared by any other group.

Most traditional symbolic clothing is either homemade or custom-made: women's dresses, bonnets, head coverings, men's hats and suits. Some clothing that is symbolic for the plain people is actually mass-produced for the general public, but the plain people specify certain distinguishing styles or patterns. For example, they do buy high, laced shoes for men and women, black stockings, metal eyeglass frames, long-sleeved shirts, and solid-color fabrics.

The Importance of Symbols

There seems to be a human need for symbolic clothing. In the course of time certain items of clothing somehow become associated with particular groups, professions, and functions. This process is often difficult to explain. In this chapter it has been demonstrated that the formation of plain clothing followed a somewhat logical path. Many other clothing symbols have no apparent logical explanation. Why did the typical man's white wig of the early 18th century become the symbol of the English judge, while the wig of the later part of the same century became the badge of the English barrister? And why did the riding coat of the last decade of the 18th century eventually become the formal evening coat? The fact that specialized or symbolic clothing often has an origin detached from its eventual association does not detract from its final significance. Most people merely acknowledge this significance and do not analyze it.

It is noteworthy that once a clothing symbol is established it often endures for a very extended period of time. Consider the ancient ceremonial costumes which abound in Europe, such as the 16th century uniforms of the Vatican Guard and uniforms of England's Yeoman of the Guard. Just as these costumes are considered timeless, so the plain people believe their dress is still a valid expression of the principles it has traditionally stood for. They are convinced it is an appropriate way to practice biblical teachings within the context of Western society.

It is possible that the formative or developmental stage of plain clothing has largely ended. In many plain groups many items of clothing have attained symbolic status. In this way change is best resisted. Those who wish to dress plain, at least within the next century or two, will probably continue to observe the established clothing symbols.

4.
The Faithful Few

Today there are over 100,000 people who, for religious reasons, continue to uphold distinctive dress standards for men and women. They are members of the Amish, Hutterites, and various conservative groups of Mennonite and Brethren, whose beginnings are all rooted in Anabaptism.

In addition, there are many other churches that had maintained plain dress until quite recently, but either gradually or abruptly dropped clothing restrictions in the 20th century. These include the Mennonite Church, the Church of the Brethren, the Brethren in Christ, several Canadian Mennonite groups of Russian background, and the conservative element in the Society of Friends (Quakers). Among the approximately 300,000 members of these churches are many people, mostly elderly and predominantly women, who still wear some type of religious garb.

Mennonites Vary in Practice

Historically, Mennonites in some areas were much stricter than others in maintaining plain dress. By the mid-19th century old forms of dress were being abandoned in many communities, especially by men. Some church leaders saw a need for more consistency in dress standards, and so, in the last decades of the 19th century, a revival of plain dress began and reached a peak from 1920 to 1940. In the West and Midwest, where the plain dress revival did not fully catch on, only a minimum of conservative dress standards were being observed in the 1950s.

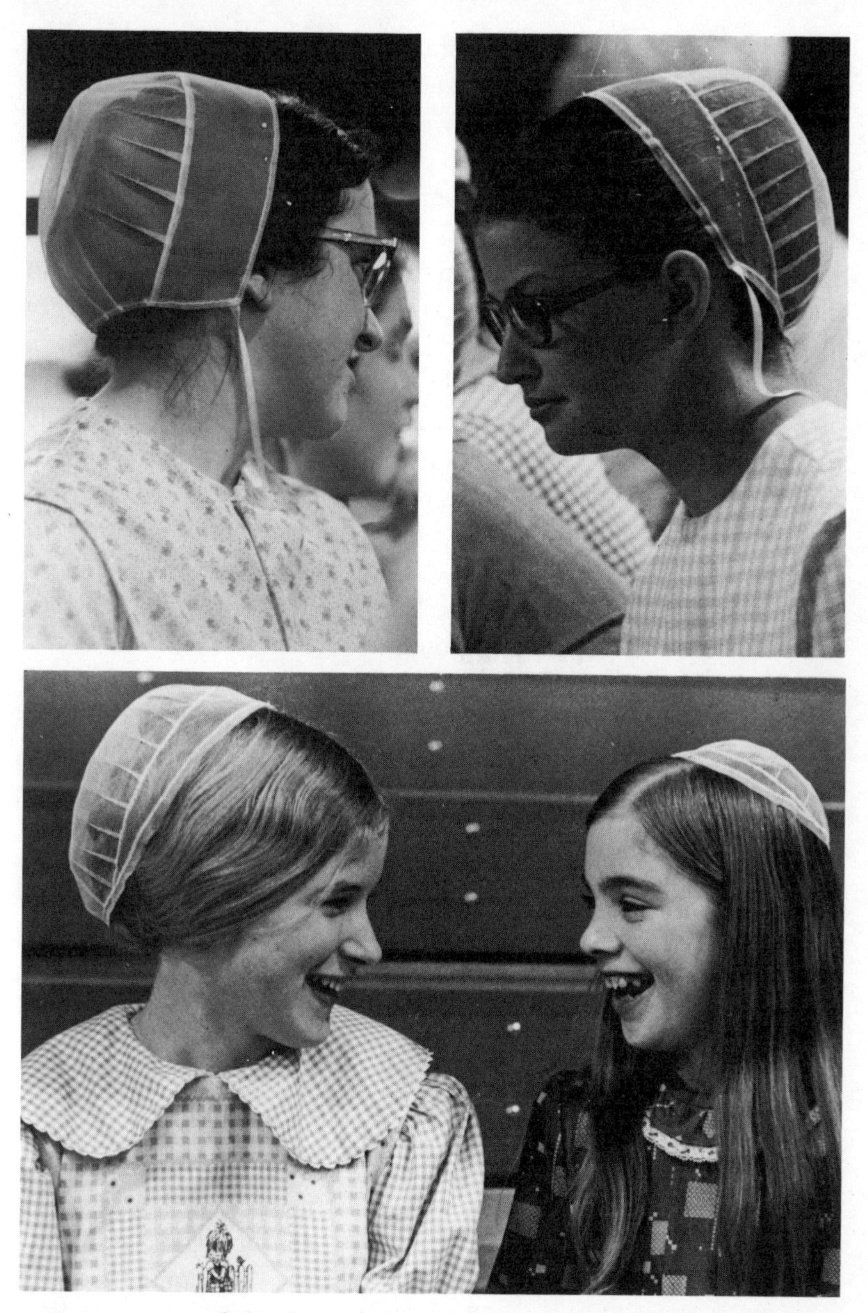

Four types of head coverings found among Lancaster County Mennonites. Upper left—Wenger Mennonite, upper right—Horning Mennonite, bottom—Lancaster Conference Mennonites.

In the large conservative Mennonite communities in the East there was a very rapid abandonment of plain clothing in the 1960s and 1970s, and by the 1980s few people under 40 were wearing it. Frequently, those who wished to preserve plain clothing withdrew from the main body of Mennonites to form small independent groups.

The Church of the Brethren made a concentrated effort to maintain plain clothing all through the 19th century. It is very likely that the Brethren provided an example for the Mennonite revival of plain dress. Ironically, when the Mennonite zeal for plainness was gaining momentum, the Brethren were rapidly casting it aside. After the withdrawal of the conservative Dunkard Brethren element in 1926, little was said officially about dress in the Church of the Brethren. Only a few congregations in Pennsylvania still retained plain dress to any degree. Most of these remained with the Church of the Brethren, but some withdrew to form very small independent groups.

The Brethren in Christ tried to avoid legislating dress regulations for most of their history but did strongly promote traditional plain clothing until recently. In the 1930s, in an effort to halt worldly drift, dress expectations were spelled out in official statements. Not all areas of the church accepted this attempt at uniformity. As the church entered into increased contact with the evangelical mainstream in the 1950s, many leaders felt plain clothing was a hindrance to their outreach. By the 1970s little was left of plain dress in the Brethren in Christ Church. Only a few very small groups withdrew from the main body to preserve the old ways.

Great Diversity

Within the same faith families described above are several groups which 1) never maintained a distinctive style of dress, 2) ceased to observe separation in the 19th century, and 3) divided from more conservative groups in objection to traditional practices including plain clothing. These religious bodies include the majority of the Society of Friends, the General Conference Mennonite Church, the Mennonite Brethren, the Brethren Church

The Plain Churches and Related Groups

Non-Plain	*Membership*
General Conference Mennonite	36,318
Conference of Mennonites in Canada	26,084
Mennonite Brethren	40,248
Evangelical Mennonite Brethren	4,081
Evangelical Mennonite Church	3,857
Missionary Church	33,259
Bible Fellowship	6,235
Brethren Church	14,229
Grace Brethren	41,733
Church of God (New Dunkards), unorganized	600*
German Seventh Day Baptist	82
Apostolic Christian (Nazarene)	2,684
Friends General Conference and Friends United Meeting	73,397
Unaffiliated Friends	5,948
Evangelical Friends Alliance	25,702
Schwenkfelder	3,001

Semi-Plain and Transitional	*Membership*
Mennonite Church (General Assembly Conferences)	100,567
Evangelical Mennonite Conference	5,400
Sommerfelder Mennonite	9,000*
Chortitza Mennonite	1,500
Reinlaender Mennonite	2,400*
Old Colony Mennonite (Canada)	3,184
Emmanuel Mennonite (Kansas)	240*
Zion Mennonite (Manitoba)	200*
New Reinland Mennnonite (Ontario)	500*
Brethren in Christ	17,367
United Zion	897
United Christian	412
Church of the Brethren	159,184
Association of Fundamental Gospel Churches (Free Brethren)	150*
(Shoemaker) Brethren in Christ Fellowship (6 churches)	?
Broadfording Bible Brethren (Maryland)	1,000*
Fundamental Brethren (North Carolina)	127
Conservative Society of Friends	1,676
Central Yearly Meeting of Friends	437
Amana Society	1,500*
Apostolic Christian	12,450
Christian Apostolic	300*

Plain	*Membership*
Old Order Amish	45,000*
Beachy Amish Mennonite	6,240
Kauffman Amish Mennonite	727
Pike Mennonite (Stauffer, etc.)	600*
Old Order Mennonite (buggy)	5,000*
Old Order Mennonite (car)	4,600*
Reformed Mennonite Conservative Mennonite (non-conference, etc.)	13,000*
Holdeman Mennonite	10,266
Kleine Gemeinde Mennonite	1,200*
Old Colony Mennonite (Latin America)	14,281
Apostolische Brudergemeinde	25*
Hutterian Brethren	13,201
Calvary Holiness	50*
Evangelical Brethren	100*
Old Order River Brethren	320
Old German Baptist	5,263
Old Brethren and Old Order German Baptist	100*
Old Brethren	150*
Dunkard Brethren	1,035*
Various conservative Brethren groups (6 bodies)	350*
German Apostolic Christian	200*
Shakers	10*

* *Estimated*

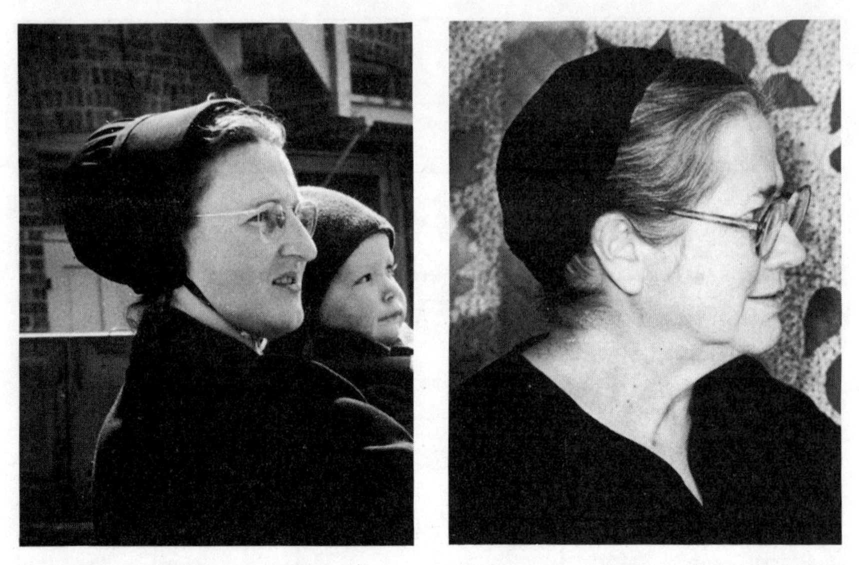

Two types of Mennonites bonnets. The woman at left is from Ontario but her bonnet is (or was) typical of several conservative groups in the U.S. The crochet bonnet at right is found among older women in the Lancaster Mennonite Conference.

(Ashland, Ohio), the Grace Brethren Church and the Missionary Church (of Mennonite background).

Plain clothing essentially disappeared in Europe by the mid-20th century. Some European groups, such as the Apostolic Christian, still practice a degree of simplicity in dress but do not have a uniform garb. The distinctively dressed Hutterian Society of Brothers also have a community in England.

Drifting Into the World

Why have so many people, including whole churches and groups who once wore plain dress, now abandoned it? The pressure to conform to mainstream society has steadily increased over the years until only the most convinced have been able to resist being outwardly assimilated. Separation from the world became more difficult when improved transportation and increased population ended physical isolation. As plain people moved from the farm and into professions, many found it difficult and embarrassing to be

The plain coat and cape dress worn by this Lancaster Conference Mennonite couple were very common among Mennonites in the East until the 1960s, but now are found mainly among the elderly and in the conservative splinter groups.

identified with a rurally oriented culture. As some plain churches began mission work in cities and foreign countries, many workers felt that plain clothing was a hindrance to their outreach.

In most cases the loss of plain clothing has been a slow erosion. One practice after another is let go until nothing is left. In some instances churches have clung to a few items of traditional dress, but eventually these have become greatly modified to conform to contemporary styles. In its final stages, the so-called plain dress is hardly discernable from worldly dress.

The Case of the Diminishing Bonnet

The bonnets worn by Mennonite women in the eastern United States have undergone considerable change during the 20th century. After 1900, the bonnet brim was gradually whittled down and the neck curtain shrank and finally disappeared. Then the ribbon ties were replaced with a chin strap that had a clasp on one side. Later, around 1940 to 1950, the bonnet was reduced to a small black "beanie" held to the back of the head with a hat pin. The last development was to make these beanie bonnets of crocheted yarn, often in a variety of colors. In the main body of the Mennonite Church today, virtually the only women who wear any kind of bonnet are those over age 40. In the various conservative Mennonite splinter groups, one may observe all the different stages of development (or disintegration) of the bonnet.

The Midwest Amish Pattern of Change

In the large Amish settlements of the Midwest there are somewhat standard patterns of change. A series of steps have been established extending from the Old Order on one side to total assimilation into the larger society on the other. Each of these positions continues to exist as some groups move to more advanced stages and more conservative groups move forward to occupy those same positions. An individual may move more rapidly by transferring from one group to another. Various groups have endeavored to halt this progression; some have been fairly successful.

Step 1. (Old Order) Men wear hats with fairly wide brims. Beards are long, usually untrimmed. Hair is cut in a "bowl" shape with bangs. Suspenders have no buckles. Shirts have no pockets. Pants are broadfalls and have no hip pockets. A vest and often a coat are worn for church services. Dress coats and vests fasten with hooks and eyes.

Women always wear an apron. A cape is worn for church and often for other occasions. Capes, and sometimes aprons, are white for Sunday church services. Head coverings are pleated on the crown and the strings are tied, at least for church. Unmarried girls wear black head coverings for church and often at other times. Small girls often wear pinafore-type aprons. Women's and girls' hair is parted in the middle and worn pinned up in a bun. Heavy black stockings are the rule for formal occasions. Large black bonnets and shawls are the preferred "going away" dress.

Step 2. Beards and hair are drastically trimmed. The hair is parted in the middle but is cut off straight in back. Hat brims become very narrow and the youth discard hats altogether. Store-bought clip-on suspenders are used. Pockets appear on pants and shirts. Wristwatches are tolerated. Store-bought zipper jackets are worn for every day. It is permissible to go without coat or vest in church.

Bonnets, shawls, white capes and aprons, elaborate pleating on head coverings, black coverings for single women, and pinafore aprons disappear. Dresses become shorter, colors brighter, and stockings thinner. Women's bib aprons appear for everyday wear.

Step 3. Beards become even more abbreviated. Suspenders are replaced with belts, and broadfalls with zipper pants.

Aprons are no longer required as a part of the formal dress. Head-covering ties may be left untied even for church.

Step 4. Beards are now optional. Haircuts are the standard tapered style. Buttons replace hooks and eyes on suit coats, and outside pockets appear.

Little girls wear their hair down in braids and do not wear head coverings until they join the church.

Step 5. Head-covering ties are now optional; printed dress fabrics are allowed. Women's hair does not need to be parted in the middle.

Step 6. Plain coats are no longer required, but neckties are still forbidden. Black stockings and capes are discarded.

This Beachy Amish Congregation in Kansas is one of many churches that withdrew from the Old Order Amish since the 1920s.

Step 7. Neckties make their appearance. Skirt-and-blouse combinations meet approval.

Step 8. Women may wear their hair down. Head coverings are worn only for church; they may be made of lace.

Step 9. Women are allowed to cut their hair. Slacks and shorts are worn by women and girls during the week. Wedding bands are permitted. Head coverings are not worn at all.

These various stages vary somewhat from one community to the next. And of course the smaller settlements do not have representative churches in each stage.

The Fight Against Fads and Fashions

From the earliest times until the present there have been many members of plain churches who have not been convinced of the value of plain clothing. Some have eventually left the plain churches while others have stayed on and instigated changes from within.

Some young people have found it especially difficult to willingly take on the church's established forms of dress. The youthful need for singularity and peer group recognition has done much to bring about changes in dress in every generation. Most of these changes have been in the direction of current fashions, but others are in-group fads that defy established standards and practices. Women's covering ties are one example. Tie strings have generally been wide among girls whose mothers wore narrow strings, and narrow when the old custom was to have wide tie strings.

Frequently, girls find ways to add fancy stitching, extra buttons, lace, ruffles and ornamental collars to their dresses. Decorative pins have been a point of contention. Boys and girls alike experiment with tight-fitting clothing, flashy watchbands, bright colors and bold patterns. Boys' hair styles often reflect contemporary fads, whether long or short. It seems that many unconvinced members of plain churches have become experts in finding loopholes in their church standards. They know which rules will not likely be enforced, and they incorporate as many fashionable accessories into their wardrobe as possible.

Many church leaders are tolerant with young people and hope that their frivolity will disappear with age and maturity.

The great variety of dress styles reflects the diversity of practice among Lancaster Conference Mennonites in the 1980s. One would not see this much conservative dress in most other Mennonite Conferences.

Sometimes this happens; in many cases, however, the styles and trends begun by the youth carry through to their adult years and become a primary source of erosion of dress standards. When each successive generation feels it must put its unique mark on the traditional dress, and few are content to dress exactly like their "old fogey" parents, there is little chance of reversal. In the end, a form of clothing may result that is either completely fashionable or that is quite unique but no longer expresses the principle it was originally intended to. Some examples of this are very tight-fitting capes on dresses, wide-brimmed black hats worn with the brims bent up on the sides, cowboy style, and "plain" clothing made from eye-catching, gaudy fabrics.

Separate Only on Sunday

Some groups have tried to halt their members' drift into fashion at a rather advanced stage. They have strongly emphasized a few surviving items of dress and made them a test of membership. The plain coat is one such item. In many conservative Mennonite and Brethren churches men are required to wear the plain coat for

The 1902 wedding photo (at left) from Lancaster, Pennsylvania illustrates the typical contrast between the level of nonconformity in dress expected of Mennonite men and women. The two young women (at right, ca. 1905) were both from Lancaster Conference Mennonite homes, but the one had not yet joined the church and, hence, did not dress in the church garb.

formal occasions, particularly Sundays, at least in cooler weather. But at other times they may wear conservative styles of conventional clothing.

Consequently, throughout the week, these men appear little different from non-plain men. Thus they easily lose their distinctiveness and they may find their occasional "separation" an embarrassment.

The Struggle for Women

In many instances in the past and present, plain women have been required to be much more nonconformed than men. Many plain women have found this to be unfair and inconsistent; in fact, for some, it has become their reason for changing to more fashionable styles.

In the 1890s Mennonite Noah Mack became convicted about this inconsistency. While traveling in their buggy, Lizzie, his wife, remarked as they passed another vehicle, "I guess they were Mennonites; she looked like it." Noah resolved that thereafter people would not know his church identity by his wife but by himself. Sometimes men have been responsible for the loss of plain clothing among women. If young men choose wives from among those young women who stretch the church's dress standards, a large percentage of girls will compromise the rules rather than risk remaining single.

Plain Becomes Popular

Sometimes popular fashions have helped to reinforce traditional practices. This occurs when plain practices and popular styles coincide. Ministers who have vehemently preached against short dresses have suddenly found their problem solved when fashion sends hemlines downward. Similarly, churches that promote but do not require the wearing of beards experience a great increase in the number of beard-wearers when beards become socially acceptable. The individualistic clothing trend has also made noncomformity in dress more acceptable to outsiders and less troublesome for insiders than was true in the conformist '50s and earlier. On the other hand, this same mood has contributed to a greater reluctance to conform to church standards.

Certain items of clothing the plain people have found impractical to manufacture themselves. Such things as hats, shoes, and eyeglasses, and the materials with which to make other clothing, are therefore prone to frequent change since they are subject to variable commercial availability. For instance, the rolled brim stiff hats traditionally worn by Lancaster Amish bishops are now very difficult to obtain. The unavailability (either real or supposed) of appropriate styles of shoes has been responsible for the acceptance of fashionable footwear in some circles. One group requires that wedge soles on women's shoes be cut down with a razor blade to form a regular heel. Amish women in Ohio have had to change the type of material they use to make their head coverings because the traditional organdy is very scarce. An ironic development occurred in the availability of old-fashioned metal frame eyeglasses which are required by many Old Order groups. These frames were difficult to obtain in the early 1960s, but when a number of popular singers started wearing them, wire rims appeared on the market again.

5.
Change: A Case Study from the Mennonite Church

The Lancaster Conference of the Mennonite Church tried to maintain plain dress much longer than most other regional Mennonite conferences. In the 1940s, the Conference still strongly stressed the principles of nonconformity. It was during this time in 1942, that the Conference established Lancaster Mennonite School (LMS) as a setting where many faith ideals could be practiced and promoted. Among these convictions were separation and humility symbolized by the wearing of plain clothing.

This four-year high school was actually in a better position to enforce dress regulations than many of the individual congregations in its constituency. Hence, through the efforts of the governing board, LMS held on to certain standards longer than the Lancaster Conference church in general.

Constituent Support Needed for Dress Code

Even in this situation, however, the school could not retain indefinitely practices not observed among the majority of the constituency. (A clear indication of the "lag" between school regulations and church expectations were the comparatively few students who continued observing the prescribed dress practices after they left school.) Changes came gradually and cautiously at first, but in one decade, the 1970s, nearly all traditional dress practices were dropped.

1949

1985

A study of the process of change at Lancaster Mennonite School provides a well-documented example of how a church group can lose its distinctive dress standards piece by piece, issue by issue, in a relatively short time. This process was repeated in many other groups at different times. It had occurred in other areas of the Mennonite Church much earlier.

The following is a chronological account of changes based on official records and publications, *The Laurel Wreath* yearbook, personal observations, and the accounts of various students and teachers.

1943—All male teachers are required to wear the regulation plain coat without a necktie. Plain coats are also recommended for male students, but lapel coats are permitted; ties are discouraged, but bow ties allowed. (In the 1940s a few students wore bow ties with plain coats.) In the classroom boys must have long shirt sleeves and these must not be rolled up; collars must be buttoned. Coats or sweaters are mandatory except during very warm weather. Gaudy designs and colors are prohibited for shirts, socks, hats, and sweaters. Long pants are to be worn by boys for all sports. Hats or caps are to be worn to and from school.

Girls' dresses are to reach halfway between knees and ankles, with full-length sleeves and capes. Black stockings are the rule. Dresses are to be of "quiet" colors; only small-print fabrics allowed. The devotional prayer covering with tie strings is required for all members of the Mennonite Church. Bonnets are to be worn to and from school.

1945—In winter boys are to wear hats or caps to and from school; in warm seasons they are "encouraged" to do so. Head coverings, designed to fit hair worn low on the back of the head, are not allowed. Dresses for Freshman and Sophomore girls must reach at lease one-third of the way between knees and ankles, or halfway on tall or mature girls.

1949—Sophomore and Freshman girls' dresses must be at least three inches below the knees; Junior and Senior girls' dresses must be at least one-third of the way between the knees and ankles. No mention is made of covering style.

1950—Eighty percent of Senior boys wear plain coats.

1959

1968

1969

1954—Covering strings are no longer required for girls. The new ruling was announced during a chapel service and some girls reportedly ripped off their covering strings immediately.

1955—Sixty-four percent of Senior boys wear plain coats. Ten out of 45 Senior girls appear to be wearing covering strings.

1958—Several new rules are introduced to counteract contemporary fads; no letters, insignias, corsages, or metal ornaments on jackets or sweaters; no flat-top, crew-cut, or ducktail hair styles for boys; no tight trousers.

No trim, lace, or buttons of contrasting color are allowed on girls' dresses. The front piece of the covering is to be at least 1¾ inches wide. Girls' hair is to be parted in the middle. (This rule was in general practice until 1954 when some girls began parting their hair on the side. Apparently, the rule was never strictly enforced, judging by pictures in the yearbook in this and subsequent years.)

No mention is made of wearing hats, caps, or bonnets to and from school. Girls are required to wear bonnets only on the senior class trip to Washington, D.C. Coats and sweaters for boys in the classroom are not specified. In hot weather, permission is given for shirt collars to be open.

1960—Fifty percent of Senior boys wear plain coats.

1961—Covering strings are no longer required for women teachers.

1963—Black stockings are not required for girls. (Before this, stockings were so sheer they were hardly recognizable as black.)

1965—Thirty percent of Senior boys wear plain coats. Girls are allowed to wear culottes for physical education class.

1968—New fads condemned: sandals, hair ribbons, pantdresses, pullover sweaters (for girls), fishnet hose, beehive hair styles. Dresses are to be long enough to completely cover the knees. Sleeves for boys and girls are to be at least elbow length. The front piece of the covering is to measure at least 1½ inches wide.

1970—Capes are not required for girls' dresses. Dresses are to be one piece or jumper and jacket combinations. Many girls wear stylish ankle-length "maxi" dresses, a trend that continued through the '70s.

1972

1982

Boys may wear long ties if they are of dark, solid colors. Seniors: nine percent of the boys wear plain coats, six percent wear bow ties, nine percent of the girls wear cape dresses.

1971—Plain-coat and cape-dress rules are dropped for teachers. Boys may wear long ties. Girls are no longer required to wear head coverings for sports.

Boys are permitted knee-length cut-offs for sports. Collarless, knit shirts are beginning to appear for boys.

1972—Bonnets are not required for the Senior trip. (Prior to this, the bonnet had diminished to a very small beanie which most girls wore for the first and only time on the trip.) Girls may wear their hair down if it is bound in a ponytail or pigtails.

Many boys now comb their hair over the tops of their ears. Boys may wear regular-length shorts for sports.

1973—Approximately half of the Senior girls wear their hair up. (For some time, many girls were getting two Senior pictures taken; one with their hair up and wearing a covering for the yearbook, and another for their own use with their hair down, with or without a covering.) Any girl without hair long enough to tie back must remain out of school until she can do so. Dresses are to reach at least to the knees (not more than three inches from floor level when kneeling erect).

1974—"Traditional white net veiling [head covering] is to be worn on campus."

1976—"Traditional two-piece veiling [head covering] is to be worn on campus." Boys' hair is not to cover the ear lobes or collar on a dress shirt.

1978—"Traditional veiling" is to be worn during school hours. Girls may wear slacks for participation in certain activities as approved by the administration. (Formerly this was only allowed if a dress or ¾-length coat was worn over the slacks.)

Teachers are allowed to wear wedding rings, but the practice is very much discouraged. Girls and women teachers may wear their hair free-flowing. Out of 99 Senior girls, 11 wear their hair up; only three wear their hair in pigtails; many have shorter hair.

1979—Boys may wear colored T-shirts (not plain white), but none with suggestive messages.

Mustaches are officially permitted for students and teachers. (Some students had worn them prior to this.)

1980—Girls do not need to wear head coverings. Eighteen coverings are visible on the portraits of 84 Senior girls. Ten of these wear their hair up. Some of the coverings are of the round lace type (chapel veils or "doilies"). (In previous years, many girls had been keeping their coverings in their lockers and wearing them only for school.)

1981—The girls' basketball uniforms now include regular shorts instead of culottes. The field hockey team now wears "kilts." Circular lace coverings appear among women teachers. Ankle socks are approved for girls. (Knee socks had been accepted for nine to 10 years.)

1982—Black or dark-colored lace coverings are now worn by many staff members.

1984—Women teachers do not need to wear coverings. Caps and gowns are first used at commencement. This innovation was said to be an effort to stop competition in clothing and to present a uniform appearance.

1986—One out of 77 Senior girls wears a covering. None wear their hair up. No Senior boys wear plain coats. One female faculty member wears a covering; none wear cape dresses. One male faculty member wears a plain coat. Girls are still not permitted to wear shorts or slacks in the classroom. Earrings are not to be worn. Those who have pierced ears try to hide the fact by wearing their earrings backward or by putting tape over the earrings. Girls are permitted to wear slacks on the senior trip.

1990—Girls are permitted to wear slacks to school, but not jeans.

6.
Who Else Dresses Plain?

Pennsylvania Dutch . . . Amish . . . Mennonite . . . Quaker . . . Shaker. To many people these names connote images of men and women wearing somber, old-fashioned, plain clothing. More than a few individuals also associate this type of appearance with Mormons. A distinctly dressed religionist might even be identified as a modern-day Pilgrim or Puritan.

Many of the plain people are of Pennsylvania Dutch (actually German) decent. But not all Pennsylvania Dutch are plain people; some have never been. Thousands of Germans found refuge in Pennsylvania in the 18th century. They and their descendants were nicknamed the Pennsylvania Dutch. But only a small number of these immigrants belonged to the plain sects. The great majority were of the Lutheran and Reformed faiths who put little or no emphasis on dress. The Moravians and Schwenkfelders were also among the Pennsylvania Dutch. Both these groups, although plain in their dress at one time, long ago gave up distinctive clothing.

A Few Plain Quakers Remain

The Quakers—or, properly, the Society of Friends—have long been the most well-known of all plain people. Their notability is probably due to their early arrival in the New World and their involvement in the affairs of colonial America. And until the mid-19th century the Friends were likely the most numerous of American plain people.

Frank Wood (1870-1962) a conservative Quaker lived the last 25 years of his life in eastern Ohio. (photo 1950s)

The few remaining Shakers still wear a distinctive garb. These two women are from the Canterbury, New Hampshire community.

Quakers emphasized proper clothing through much of their history, although distinctive plain clothing was generally only practiced by those who felt a personal inspiration to wear it. (In the conservative circles one's testimony was not taken seriously unless he or she had this inspiration and no one was considered for positions of leadership without it.) There were always plain Quakers and fancy Quakers. By the late 19th century plain Quakers were largely found only in the Conservative (Wilburite) Yearly Meetings in the Midwest and in the independent Philadelphia (Arch Street) Yearly Meeting. In these bodies, plain Friends were quite numerous into the 20th century, but by the 1950s only a small remnant remained.

The Shakers, though never large in number, have received a great deal of public attention. Simple, modest clothing has been a Shaker trademark. Present day Shakers—there are fewer than a dozen—continue to wear the characteristic dress.

The austere clothing associated with the Pilgrims and Puritans of New England was not really a religious sectarian garb. There were rigid dress codes in early Massachusetts, but these did not become part of the tradition of the Puritans' spiritual descendants, the Congregationalists.

It is difficult to understand why so many people associate plain clothing with Mormons. It is true that Brigham Young had a great deal to say about dress and even prescribed a special costume for women. But few members ever followed his advice. Perhaps many people assume that since Mormons have unique beliefs they should also have a unique style of dress. Actually, Mormons do have special ritual garments, but these are not seen by outsiders. A very small Mormon splinter group, the Order of Aaron, has adopted a uniform garb for women.

Holiness and Pentecostal Movements

Apart from the distinctly plain groups a large number of North American churches observe regulations concerning personal appearance. The Holiness movement, which sprang out of 19th century Methodism, developed stringent dress codes. As the Holiness movement grew and modernized, a number of smaller groups saw the need to organize separately in order to keep the old

This group from People's Bible College (started by the Emmanuel Association) in Colorado represents some of the most conservative dress within the Holiness movement.

ways. Matters considered essential to the sanctified appearance were uncut hair and modestly long dresses for women. Makeup, jewelry, and slacks were forbidden to female members. Both sexes were to wear long sleeves, and men were to keep their hair respectably short.

A number of Pentecostal bodies share some of all of the Holiness characteristics of appearance as do some groups of Old Regular Baptists, Plymouth Brethren, Christian Fellowship (from Ireland and Scotland), Apostolic Lutherans, and others.

Among Russian Old Believers, Molokans, and Doukhobors one will find some forms of traditional dress. The old-fashioned Russian costumes might be worn daily or just for special occasions, depending on the custom of the individual congregation.

Catholic Orders and Jewish Traditions

Some of the same ideals of asceticism are shared by the plain people and various Protestant and Catholic religious orders. Indeed, away from their home environment, plain people are often mistaken for nuns or priests and vice versa. One group of plain girls from Pennsylvania took the train to visit friends in Iowa.

These Carmelite nuns wear the traditional habits of their order. Most Catholic sisters modified or discarded their religious garb after the 1960s.

The beards and black hats of Hasidic Jewish men make them easily mistaken for plain men. The skull caps and locks of hair at the temples are other Hasidic symbols.

Since there was a long layover in Chicago, they decided to take a taxi to see some of the sights. The taxi driver, thinking they might be nuns, asked, "Are you sisters?" One of the girls misunderstood the nature of the question, replied, "No, but some of us are cousins."

When away from home, plain men with black hats and beards have often been greeted with "Shalom," reflecting the striking resemblance between Old Order plain men and Hasidic (ultra-orthodox) Jews. There is also an interesting parallel in the Jewish man's *yarmulke* (skull cap) and the plain woman's head covering. In the moderately conservative factions of both groups, one sex wears a religious symbol constantly while the other sex is free to blend in with the surrounding culture.

7. Common Objections to Plain Dress

Many objections of both a practical and a religious nature have been given for not wearing distinctive plain clothing. The following are some typical examples, followed by explanations the plain people give in support of their practices.

1. How do you ever stand all that clothing? Isn't it too hot and uncomfortable?

We wish to maintain scriptural and traditional standards of decency and modesty even though this might cause us to perspire. For centuries all people in the civilized world wore as much or more clothing than do present plain people. If former generations found no problem in being fully clothed, we shouldn't either. The current trend toward scanty attire hardly came about because of climatic changes. We do not support the idea, "If it feels good, do it," in dress, or in any other area of life.

2. Plain clothing might be all right for farmers and other rural people, but it hardly seems feasible for a modern urban dweller.

Hasidic Jews, who are very distinctive in their dress, have thrived in the New York City metropolis.

3. What is wrong with the dress of today's youth? It's simple, comfortable, and unpretentious.

The casual dress of modern youth may be unassuming, but it is also symbolic of the relaxed morals of this age. We do not wish to be associated with that trend.

Amish—Ontario.

4. What about cheap, second-hand clothing from thrift shops and garage sales? It's economical and usually not in the latest fashion.

Yes, but it is often representative of brief extreme fads which are unsatisfactory to plain people.

5. Plain clothing can be very expensive, especially men's suits. Doesn't that defeat the purpose of simplicity?

Some men have their plain suits professionally custom-tailored. It is true that this can be expensive. However, since the plain coat is not affected by changing styles, it usually has a much longer life than a fashionable coat. Most Old Order plain people have always made their own suits and many of the more moderate groups are now turning to this practice. Women's plain clothing is nearly all made at home.

6. Isn't plain clothing just "frozen" styles which were once fashionable in the "world?"

Some items of plain clothing may have been worn by non-plain people at one time (although that does not mean it was necessarily fashionable). However, it seems that the formation of plain dress was a selective process and not simply an arbitrary one. By studying the history of each item of plain clothing it appears that there were good reasons why each was adopted. Some items originated among simple country folk, some were associated with periods of increased morality and religious awakening, other garments appealed because of their simple design. (The plain people often further simplified them). In any case, the plain people were not constantly changing their clothing to conform to popular fashions. Once they decided that a particular item of dress was appropriate they continued to use it indefinitely.

7. A distinctive sectarian dress would severely limit a person's choice of occupations.

Many plain people have not let plain clothing become a hindrance in the business and professional world. Instead, these people feel that their dress has helped them to maintain Christian ethics. They feel that if they cannot wear plain clothing in a particular job, that is a good indication that such a job is not appropriate for a Christian.

Old Order Mennonite—Ontario.

8. Plain clothing brings a stigma to the wearer which is psychologically damaging.

A person can have real personal satisfaction in belonging to a brotherhood and supporting its standards. Outward identification with a group of separated Christians does not usually create a problem unless one is not convicted of the ideals of the group.

9. A uniform garb injures one's sense of self-worth. People should feel good about themselves and be free to make themselves as attractive as possible.

Knowing that one is doing God's will gives any person a sense of personal worth. Contentment with the way God has made one is also important. Artificial beauty aids do not accentuate the inner beauty spoken of in the Bible. Simple attire allows personal virtue to shine through. Creativity is only constructive when it is used in a way that pleases God.

10. How can Christians justify quibbling over minute dress details when there are so many more important needs which don't get sufficient attention?

If we are not careful to keep ourselves outwardly separate from the world, we will soon become absorbed into the world's system.

Then we will have many more problems which will divide our attention.

11. Some preachers have constantly dwelt on dress and have wearied their audience, so that the people no longer care.

Other preachers have favorite themes such as drugs or drink. That doesn't give anyone an excuse to become an alcoholic or a drug addict.

12. It is not necessary to have a special cut of dress in order to meet scriptural standards. Plenty of clothing, which is quite appropriate for Christians, can be found in stores.

To rely completely on the mass market for one's dress seems risky. There is no guarantee that sensible clothing will always be readily available. The only way to avoid a drift toward unacceptable fashions is for the church to prescribe a uniform dress, and for most of that clothing to be made at home.

13. If a person is a true "born again" Christian, the dress question will take care of itself. Rules and regulations aren't necessary for the Spirit-filled child of God.

This is the ideal situation but it seldom happens in real life. The influences of the world are very strong. It is the church's responsibility to provide guidelines to help its members not weaken in their faith.

14. But the Bible doesn't give specifics on how Christians should dress. Man-made dress regulations are, "teaching for doctrine the commandments of men" (Matthew 15:9).

The details of dress are not matters of doctrine but are a means of expressing and maintaining scriptural teachings on modesty, simplicity, and separation. The danger is that if the church supplies only general suggestions on this matter, the world will fill in with fashionable specifics.

15. Rules on dress are a form of legalism.

There are few churches that do not apply scriptural principles to issues not expressly mentioned in the Bible. The plain people apply Bible teachings to more areas of life, including dress, than most churches do. Just as civil magistrates and parents need no proof texts to back up their laws and rules, so the plain people believe

Old German Baptist annual meeting.

their churches may establish guidelines on dress for the benefit of their members. These guidelines do not replace the Bible but interpret it as the church feels it applies today.

16. In Galatians 5:11 it says, "Stand fast therefore in the liberty wherewith Christ hath made us free, and be not entangled again with the yoke of bondage." As Christians, we are free, and we have liberty. Rules and regulations about dress are bondage.

It is clear that in Galatians the apostle Paul was referring to bondage in the old law of Moses. He certainly wasn't saying Christians can do anything they please. That would contradict all the guidelines for a godly life that Paul wrote elsewhere. We are indeed free from sin but we are not free to sin. Fashionable, immodest dress is sinful. In the same chapter it says, "Use not liberty as occasion to the flesh" (verse 13). In other words, don't use your liberty as an excuse to sin.

17. Romans 12:2 says, "Be not conformed to this world but be ye transformed by the renewing of your mind." Doesn't that refer to one's thoughts and attitudes rather than one's dress?

Transformed Christians use their minds in selecting clothing as well as in any other conscious actions or decisions.

18. The Bible says, "Man looketh on the outward appearance but the Lord looketh on the heart" (I Samuel 16:7). It is what's

Amish—Pennsylvania.

in the heart that counts. God isn't really concerned about what we wear. Why all this fuss about dress when it really doesn't matter?

A heart that is right won't produce wrong behavior. One judges a fruit tree by its outward appearance, not by cutting it down and examining the "heart" of the wood. To "abstain from all appearance of evil" (I Thessalonians 5:22) applies to dress as well as all outward behavior. If what we wear doesn't matter, then anything we do will not matter either.

19. Christ condemned the scribes and Pharisees for their outward show in order to get recognition (Matthew 23:5; Luke 20:46).

Christ also condemned ostentation in praying, fasting, and giving alms. God is concerned with our attitudes in all these matters.

20. God doesn't want us to call attention to ourselves by wearing clothing which is radically different from those around us. We want to glorify Christ, not ourselves.

Yes, plain clothing does attract attention, but any kind of right behavior stands out in the midst of evil. We do not believe we should blend in with the crowd for fear of inviting the gaze of the world. We can give Christ the glory as the source of our separated appearance and our separated conduct.

21. Because of their dress, the plain people are often identified merely as an ethnic group or folk culture rather than a body of Christians.

Our ethnic and cultural heritage has been an effective means of separating us from mainstream society and its evils. For the most part, our way of life is a kind of counter-culture based on Christian principles.

22. Plain clothing is a hindrance in witnessing for Christ. People are turned off by a holier-than-thou appearance.

There are few plain people who cannot tell of incidents in which strangers have asked about the significance of their clothing. Such occasions give many opportunities to speak of deeper spiritual matters.

23. It is obvious that a large number of those who dress in plain clothing are lacking in real Christianity. Their conduct is certainly not consistent with their pious appearance.

Yes, there are wolves in sheep's clothing, to be sure. But it does not seem any more consistent to be sheep in wolves' clothing. We prefer to be sheep in sheep's clothing.

24. Christ dressed like everyone else in his day.

Christ dressed as every other Jew, but not like a Roman, Samaritan or other non-Jew. How did the Samaritan woman at the well recognize him as a Jew (John 4:9)?

The "hem" of his garment that the afflicted woman touched to be healed (Matthew 9:20) was the distinctive border Jews were commanded to put on their garments in Numbers 15:38, 39. Even today the most orthodox Jews wear distinctive clothing.

25. If you want to be so biblical about your dress, why not wear long robes like Christ and the disciples?

If we had originated in the Middle East and continued to live in that land and culture, we probably would be wearing robes. Since our heritage is European, we feel our dress best expresses nonconformity within our own culture and is practical for the land in which we live.

8.
My Path to Plainness

In my early teens, during a series of revival meetings at a Baptist church, all four members of my family experienced Christian conversion. We had attended church only sporadically before that time. As a new believer, I enthusiastically studied what the Bible had to say about the conduct of the true Christian.

When I observed other professing Christians at school, it seemed that many did not look or act the part of a child of God. I concluded that the scripture which says, "Be not conformed to this world," took more than just inner beliefs. It did not seem consistent for a follower of Jesus Christ to imitate all the fads and fashions of secular society. I thought people would be more conscious of their Christian commitments if they were obviously different from the crowd. Various guidelines in the Bible showed me what these differences might be.

Experimenting with Nonconformity

At first I expressed nonconformity through an "old-fashioned" appearance. I bought out-of-style, wide neckties at the Goodwill store and tried to find loose-fitting trousers (this was the era of skinny ties and skin-tight, white Levis). I usually wore a vest with a large watch in one pocket and a chain draped from a buttonhole.

One group of "greasers" used to taunt me from their hallway hangout in the morning. "Hey man, got the time?" But I also received a compliment from one of the class "cool guys," who paused in front of my desk in the finger-snapping cadence across

Stephen Scott, author of Why Do They Dress That Way?

the study hall and remarked, "Heeey, cool set of threads you got there."

Later, I received inspiration and direction from those churches which had made Christian separation a part of their group witness. Occasionally, when my family visited nearby Dayton, Ohio, I caught glimpses of distinctly dressed people passing by on the streets. My parents told me they were "Dunkards." I admired the long beards and black hats of the men and the modest dresses and bonnets of the women.

As a Christian I developed a new interest in these people. I searched through books in the local library for information about the plain people, as I found they were called, and subscribed to magazines published by the various groups. I became convinced that these people were following the teachings of the Bible.

Then I persuaded my parents to include Lancaster County, Pennsylvania, on one of our vacation trips. When I began driving, I made many excursions to nearby plain communities in Ohio. I became acquainted with members of many different groups and eventually worshiped and worked with them. I was generally treated quite warmly and made many lasting friendships. I did find, however, that the plain people were just as human as anyone else, and I was often disappointed by their inconsistencies. But this discovery did not distract me from the principles and ideals of the groups, which I believed were honorable and true.

Early in this period of seeking I discovered an Old German Baptist (or Dunkard, as local folks called them) clothing store. I bought a wide-brimmed hat, broadfall pants, and suspenders. I admit I didn't wear these items too often at first. Once I donned my black hat to visit a German Baptist bake shop. I wanted to declare my identification with these people. I didn't realize until later how inconsistent my hat and my high school ring were.

One of the first changes in dress I made was to get rid of my necktie. This caused some problems at the Baptist college I attended because ties were required at the evening meal. One time I compromised by wearing a friend's wool scarf around my neck. Later I found the college authorities to be understanding of my convictions. My roommate did persuade me that I just had to wear a tie for the yearbook picture. This was after I started wearing a beard (which was also a very controversial matter at that time). So the unlikely combination of an Amish-inspired beard and a fashionable necktie are permanently recorded on the pages of the Cedarville College yearbook.

Finding a Group to Belong To

As a suburban boy, I did not have a permanent source of work on the farm like most other plain people. One year in desperation after seeking a job at many different places, I tried an employment bureau. The lady behind the big desk told me I would stand a much better chance if I would buy a snappy sport jacket and get rid of my suspenders. Eventually I avoided this problem by finding employment among the plain people themselves.

My search for Christian fellowship took me to many different churches: Mennonite, Conservative Mennonite, Beachy Amish, and all the Brethren groups in southwestern Ohio. I found admirable qualities in each church and adopted many of their convictions as my own. In 1969, when I was 21, I affiliated with the Old Order River Brethren in Lancaster County, Pennsylvania, a plain church I have appreciated and supported to the present time.

9.
Will Plain Dress Survive?

Will New World plain people eventually forsake their distinctive dress as their European brethren did? No doubt some groups and many individuals now wearing plain clothing will give up this practice in the future. History is apt to repeat itself. It seems likely, however, that plain dress as we now know it will continue at least for another several centuries. The depth of conviction on nonconformity in dress shows few signs of diminishing in the near future. Too many people are convinced of its value in identifying the community of believers and its scriptural basis.

Will Plain Clothing Change?

No group has been entirely successful in preventing change in dress. Those who have done the best in controlling change have taken the attitude that there shall be no change. Despite that, change has come even in these groups, but it has been gradual and minimal. When a group takes the attitude, "Change is inevitable, so, why fight it," the survival of plain clothing seems doubtful.

The Importance of Symbols

While changes have occurred in plain clothing down through the years, once an item attains primary symbolic status it is less likely to change. It has taken many years to establish the various elements of plain dress as symbols. Some current plain clothing symbols date back 300 years. Few symbols have become established in the last half century. If no new symbols are

Those groups that have been most successful in controlling change have taken the attitude that there shall be no change. (Amish—Ohio)

The polka dot head scarves of Hutterite women are a distinctive group symbol. (Lehrerleut from Saskatchewan)

introduced and the old symbols survive, then plain clothing will stay basically the same for an indefinite period of time.

Levels of Symbolism

Each group of plain people has a different set of dress symbols. What is an important symbol to one group may be of no importance to another group. Hooks and eyes are very essential to Old Order Amish identity but have not been observed by Old Order Mennonites. Black bonnets are important to many Amish and Mennonites but have no meaning to Hutterites.

Within each group there appears to be several levels of dress symbols. Primary symbols are required of all members and are

Levels of Symbolism in Men's Clothing			
GROUP	**PRIMARY SYMBOLS** *Required of all members*	**SECONDARY SYMBOLS** *In the best order but not required*	**MINOR SYMBOLS** *Observed by the elderly and the very conservative*
Old Order Amish (Lancaster)	T Hat with at least 3 1/4" brim T Beard after marriage T Hair cut in bangs T Plain coat and vest with hooks T Broadfall pants T,C Suspenders T,C Shirt with no pockets C Black lace shoes (for dress) C Solid colored fabrics	T Suspenders without buckles C High-top shoes	T Hat with 4" brim T Cape overcoat T Pullover shirt with 4 buttons
Old Order Mennonite (Wenger)	T Plain frock coat and vest (after marriage) T Broadfall pants (for church) T Hat T,C Suspenders C Black lace shoes (for dress)	T Hat with plain crown C High-top shoes C Metal frame glasses	T Broadfall work pants T Hat with 3" or more brim
Conservative Mennonite (Eastern PA and Fellowship)	T Plain sack coat C Long-sleeved shirt with collar buttoned C Loose-fitting trousers C Black shoes (for dress)	T Plain hat	T,C Suspenders T Frock Coat
Old Colony Mennonite (Latin America)	C Bib overalls C Hat C Dark conventional suit C Long-sleeved shirt		T Black flat cap T Frock coat *(only for ministers)* C Black shirt T High boots *(only for ministers)*
Old German Baptist Brethren	T Plain hat T Blocked hair T Plain frock coat T Vest T Broadfall pants	T Beard	T,C Suspenders

T—Traditional custom-made clothing
C—Conventional clothing with certain restrictions

The beard is an important religious symbol to Holdeman Mennonites.

Old Colony Mennonites, who have lived in Mexico since the 1920s, have retained a distinctive garb.

The birth rate in Old Order families is very high, and since a large percentage of their children remain true to the church, continued population growth is ensured.

considered essential to the identity of the group. Secondary symbols are not tests of membership but are observed by all those wishing to be in good order. Minor symbols were formerly primary or secondary symbols that gradually lost their importance and are only practiced by the very old or very conservative.

Some groups regard nearly every item of apparel as a primary symbol. These are the people who will most likely continue to be plain for many years to come. Those groups which have allowed primary symbols to slip into the secondary and minor stages seem more likely to be threatened by eventual assimilation. Those groups which observe only a few symbols are on the verge of losing all distinction.

10. General Clothing Details

Color

The popular belief is that plain people wear only somber, dark colors, preferably black or gray. In real practice, most groups allow a great deal of color in their clothing. It is true that many plain churches advise their members to wear quiet, subdued tones, but this is subject to widely varying interpretations.

The Amish insist that all clothing be made of only solid-colored fabrics. But the colors used in many Amish communities are quite bright. Purple has been a favorite of the Lancaster County Amish women. Blue is perhaps the most common in many areas, and red is not unknown (although this is strongly condemned in some Amish groups and even among Mennonite groups that are otherwise less traditional than the Amish). The Old Order Amish seldom use pink, yellow, and orange.

The Use of Prints

Mennonites, Hutterites, and Brethren groups have allowed patterned fabrics. Some say prints do not show dirt as easily. The more conservative groups specify that the figures and patterns be small. But some other very conservative people permit bold plaids and flowered fabrics. Some Hutterites have resorted to making simple designs with liquid embroidery on solid-colored fabrics when appropriate patterns were no longer available.

The girls (top) from New Wilmington, Pennsylvania, demonstrate the exclusive use of solid-colored fabrics by the Amish. The Hutterite children (bottom, Lehrerleut from Saskatchewan) show their group's preference for patterned material.

Black—A Debatable Color

Black is used for some items of plain apparel. Today, black suits for men are typical in many plain communities. But this was not always true. In the 19th century there was widespread sentiment that black was a fashionable or worldly color. During this period, black was quite popular for formal wear but as brighter shades become popular in the larger society, the plain people began seeing black as appropriate for a sober appearance.

Among the Lancaster Amish, gray was the preferred color for men's suits in the earlier part of this century, and before that brown was most typical. The Amish of Ohio preferred navy blue suits until the last 20 years but have now switched mostly to black. The LaGrange County, Indiana and New Wilmington, Pennsylvania Amish still wear gray suits, and the Nebraska Amish of Pennsylvania have kept the brown tradition for men's coats and pants (although blue and gray are also seen).

The brown custom probably originates from the early use of readily available natural dyes, such as butternut, to color homespun fabrics. For centuries, russet (reddish or yellowish brown) was the characteristic color for farmers. Eighteenth century Moravian men were usually pictured wearing brown coats. Some plain people, including a few Quakers, thought that any use of dyes was unnecessary and insisted on natural, undyed fabrics.

Black is the usual approved color for shoes, stockings (although not necessary for work), men's felt hats, and women's bonnets and shawls. Lancaster Amish and the Hutterites have used black for men's work clothing (most others prefer blue denim). In some areas, women traditionally wear black for times of mourning and for communion services. A black cap is the symbol for a single girl in most Amish communities, but among the Old Colony Mennonites the unmarried wear white head shawls and the married women wear black. Similarly, Old Order Mennonite married women have black tie strings on their white caps while single girls wear white strings.

Old Order Mennonites allow only gray wedding dresses. White for the bride is considered worldly by most Old Orders and also impractical since such special white dresses can be worn only one time. The Reinland Mennonites of Manitoba withdrew from the

The dress of the "Nebraska" Amish woman (left) and the Old Order River Brethren woman (right) are in many respects very similar. There are more differences in the dress of the men.

Sommerfelder Church when, among other things, the latter group began tolerating white wedding dresses.

The Wide and the Narrow

The width and length of various items of clothing are highly symbolic to the plain people. Among most Old Orders, "wideness" indicates conservatism when it comes to hat and bonnet brims, the front piece of a woman's cap, the peplum on the dresses of some groups, and suspenders. Ample length is traditional for women's dresses, men's beards and hair, and the height of shoe tops (for both men and women). On the other hand, "narrow" is plain in hat bands, apron strings, and cuffs on men's shirts.

Jewelry

In nearly all plain churches, jewelry is excluded, including wedding bands. Some say that it is God and not a ring that should bind husband and wife together. And in closely knit, plain communities where marriage to outsiders is forbidden, the need to demonstrate one's marital status is minimal.

Wristwatches are considered jewelry in many plain churches.

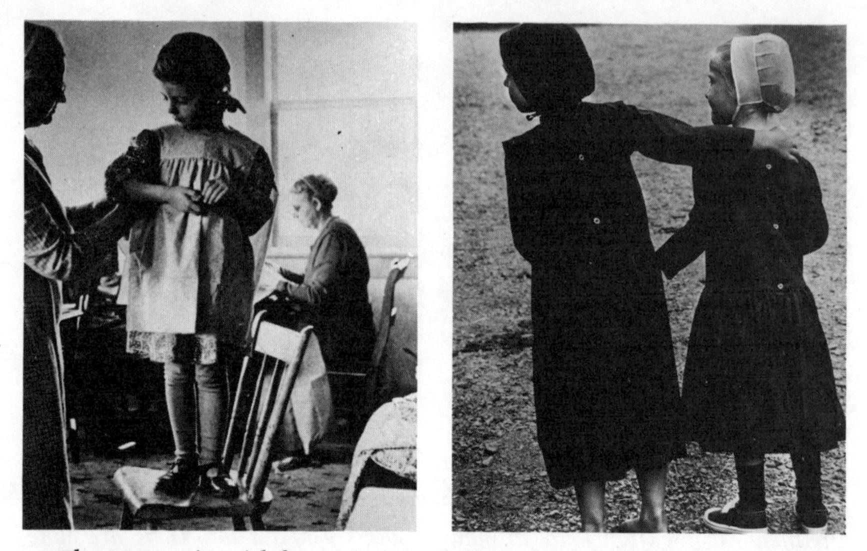

The Mennonite girl from Virginia (left) is dressed simply, but not in the full church garb. The Amish girls from Ohio (right, from two different groups) appear in traditional garb as their church interprets the scripture, "Train up a child in the way he shall go."

Old-fashioned pocket watches are the approved Old Order timepiece, but the use of fancy fobs and chains by some are thought to defeat the purpose of this practice. Some conservative Mennonites and Beachy Amish allow wristwatches but specify that they have plain non-metallic bands so they are not mistaken for bracelets. (At least one conservative Mennonite group feels so strongly about not using gold that they have it removed by a jeweler from their eyeglass frames.)

Strangely enough, among some very plain Old Order groups one will see numerous individuals wearing homemade copper rings and wrist bands. These are supposedly worn not as jewelry, but as a folk remedy to ward off arthritis.

That Which Is Unseen

Some plain groups have very definite regulations on appropriate underwear. Understandably these rules are rather difficult to enforce (would examining wash lines be the answer?). Current styles of underwear are really quite recent, and, as in other matters, plain people have retained older styles. Briefs for men and women were not popular in America until the 1930s. The most traditional Old Orders have insisted that underpants have legs (these are necessarily often made at home). Brassieres, which date back only to about the 1920s, have not found acceptance among the ultraconservatives. Any kind of lacy, fancy underwear is proscribed by the most rigid Old Orders. Plain slips are made commercially by several Old Order women.

The more moderate groups have few if any requirements in these areas. One conservative Mennonite group does feel that men should wear T-shirts rather than undershirts with straps. One member stated that women would never be permitted to have the straps of their undergarments showing through their dresses.

Some groups prefer nightgowns and nightshirts to pajamas. They also stress that women not indulge in fancy trimmings on sleepwear which would not be permitted in daytime clothing.

Maternity Clothes

A few plain groups permit specially-styled maternity clothing. Others merely make the regular clothing a little larger. In the latter case, groups that have traditionally used straight pins to fasten dresses can easily adjust to changing body contours.

Maternity tops have been a controversial matter in some of the more moderate churches. One congregation spent many long council sessions debating this issue.

Another church concluded that maternity tops were not to be permitted because their use publicly announced the condition they were designed to conceal. "We believe our regularly approved dress pattern can be made to conceal abnormal body lines just as adequately, less conspicuously, and more consistently," reasoned the Mountain View Amish Mennonites of Somerset County, Pennsylvania, in 1980.

The Example of Ministers

There is no special garb designated for the clergy in the plain churches, but often a minister can be identified by his clothing. This apparently contradictory statement can be explained by the fact that plain ministers usually wear what is considered a good model for others to follow. Often very few people actually follow this example, thus making clear-cut the differences in appearance between laity and clergy.

When a man is ordained, he wishes to demonstrate his support of the church standards and may "over-conform" to create an extra measure of confidence. Often the outward forms expected of a minister are really the old styles once worn by all members.

Among most Old Order Mennonites the ministers are expected to wear broadfall pants, and, in the groups who drive buggies, a cape overcoat. Old Colony Mennonite ministers in Latin America appear in frock coats of the Prince Albert style, black shirts, high leather boots, and special black caps.

Amish ministers generally wear wider hat brims than other men. In Lancaster, Pennsylvania, the minimum hat brim width for the non-ordained is 3¼" while the ministers have 4" brims. "Nebraska" or "white top" Amish ministers wear a distinctive blue-gray suit while others wear brown. For Old German Baptist preachers, beards are mandatory, but lay members are only urged to follow this practice (most do).

In the Mennonite Church of the 1930s and '40s, all ministers were required to wear a plain coat. In the West where few laymen wore the plain coat, it became somewhat of a clerical coat. In the East where a large percentage of men wore plain sack coats, the ordained wore the older style plain frock coats. Hutterite ministers wear long frock coats, at least for special occasions.

The wives of ministers are also expected to dress more conservatively than other women in the same church. When an unfamiliar woman visits in a Lancaster Amish church service, other women look at her shoes to see if she is a minister's wife since preachers' wives wear the old-style high shoes. Until the 1960s the wives of Lancaster Conference Mennonite ministers were expected to have aprons on their dresses.

Children

Following a very old practice, many Old Order boy babies wear dresses, a custom which appears to be fast dying out, even among comparatively traditional groups. Formerly, boys wore dresses at least until they were out of diapers. That was really the idea of the

Amish boys have traditionally worn dresses until they are out of diapers. (Ontario)

dress: it made diaper-changing easier. Now among moderate Old Order, dresses appear on boys for only a few months. In some circles, boys have worn and still do wear bonnets, mantles, and even pinafore aprons.

Some very traditional Old Orders have not adopted the use of ready-made rubber pants for babies. Instead they fold pieces of plastic over the diaper.

The Amish have stressed that children should be dressed in the full order of the church. There is widespread deviation from this practice, however. In some of the larger communities, wayward teenage Amish (mostly boys) dress "worldly" until they decide to join the church. While working in an Amish community, this writer met a young man working for a carpenter crew who, though he spoke Pennsylvania Dutch, looked like a typical American youth with his sleeveless shirt and blue jeans. Some time later the writer saw this same person in a restaurant with an Amish hat, beard, and broadfall pants. Some disobedient Amish youth live dual lives and change into fashionable dress at service stations before engaging in their merriment. Many of the newly-established small communities have come into existence primarily to avoid this kind of behavior.

The Brethren, River Brethren, and many Mennonites have not emphasized dressing their children in the full uniform garb of adults. They feel that an unconverted youth should not be expected to wear Christian clothing. Children in these groups are often dressed modestly and simply in such a way that they look somewhat old-fashioned and, hence, nonconformed. Pig tails and simple dresses for girls and short haircuts and long pants for boys are typical. In most of these groups, a girl does not wear a head covering until she experiences conversion.

Dress in Death

Even in death, the plain people have preserved traditional dress practices. The Old Order Mennonites and, to a lesser extent, the Old German Baptists and Old Order River Brethren have observed the custom of dressing the dead in shrouds. This is a long, loosely fitting, white, gown-like garment for men and women. The women's version has a cape.

Among the Lancaster County Amish, women are dressed in white dresses of the usual Amish pattern. The white capes and aprons which they wore at their wedding are used again for their funerals. Lancaster Amish men are dressed in regular white shirts and specially made white vests and pants. Deceased men of the Holmes County Amish are dressed in regular suits, and the women appear in black dresses. Babies are dressed in white; older women are sometimes buried in white also.

Old Order women generally wear black dresses when attending funerals. The Lancaster Amish have a detailed code on the length of time one wears black as a sign of mourning: a whole year for a spouse, parent, child, brother or sister; a half-year for a grandparent or grandchild; three months for an uncle, aunt, niece or nephew, and six weeks for a first cousin.

Where Do They Get Their Clothing?

The most conservative Old Orders make nearly all their own clothing. Shoes, stockings, and men's felt hats are the exceptions. These three items, plus yard goods in appropriate colors as well as buttons, hooks and eyes, and suspenders are sold in dry goods stores catering to the special needs of the plain people.

In 1862, Bishop David Beiler of Lancaster, Pennsylvania, lamented that the Amish were no longer producing their own homespun fabric. This was at the end of the period in which nearly all rural

Since the late 19th century some companies have specialized in making plain clothing. This ad is from 1902.

people switched to factory-produced cloth. The plain people have had little to say about the source of content of the fabric they use. Synthetics are now quite common. There is some warning about fabric that is too expensive, however.

Some men in the moderate plain groups have their plain suits made by custom tailors. In recent years the plain people themselves have taken up this occupation. Until the 1960s in Lancaster County, Pennsylvania, ready-made plain suits could be bought from racks in at least three different clothing department stores.

In many plain communities, seamstresses have made a business of providing men's suits and women's bonnets and head coverings. These items require special sewing skills.

Some people resort to buying factory-made clothing and modifying it to meet their standards. Conventional suit coats are altered to a standing collar plain coat in many conservative Mennonite and Brethren groups. Zipper pants are made into broadfalls by Beachy Amish and some Old Order Brethren. Some Amish remove the pockets from ready-made shirts.

11. Women's Clothing

The Cape

The cape or "hals duch" (neck cloth) of plain women is derived from the kerchief worn by European women as early as the 16th century.[1] Originally it was a square piece of cloth folded into a triangle. Later it was cut in a triangular shape. The kerchief was placed around the neck and over the shoulders like a small, lightweight shawl. One point extended down the back and the other two points were either pinned straight down the front or were crossed over each other and pinned at the waist.

The kerchief or cape is worn by nearly all plain women from all the various groups. It is also found in many surviving folk costumes of western Europe. Its wide appeal to pious country women is no doubt based on the modesty it provides. The extra covering is seen to conceal the neckline and the form of the bosom and provides privacy when nursing a baby. A 19th century English woman remarked on the Shaker woman's cape, "Certainly the most ingenious device ever contrived for concealing all personal advantage."[2]

The cape is worn in its original triangular form by some Old Order groups. It is often give a cut-out neckline and a more tailored form in less traditional groups. Other modifications which developed in some circles were the gradual blunting of the points which, in the most modern form, are cut off square and sewn to a belt or directly to the dress. Sometimes the opening comes partway down the front

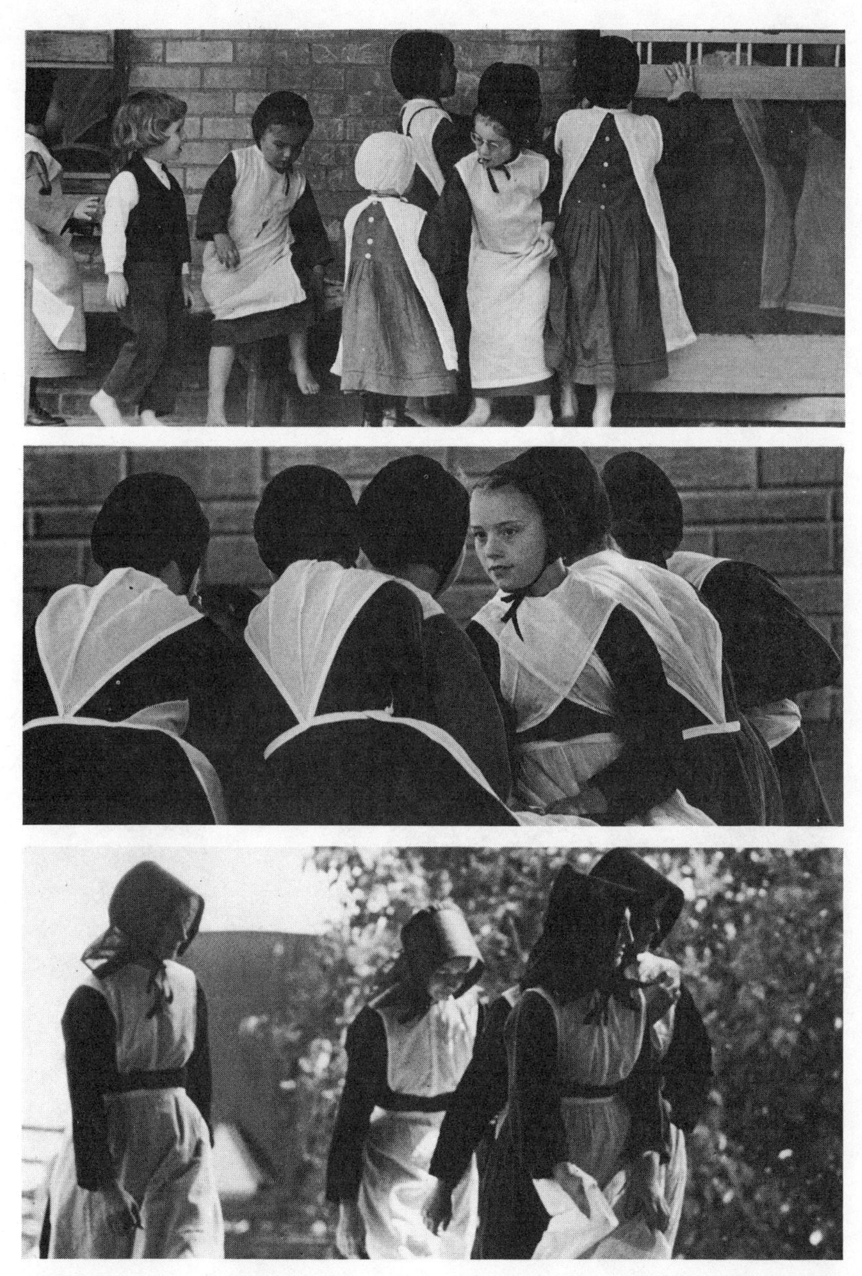

This series of pictures illustrates the changes that girls from Amish communities with Holmes County, Ohio, roots will make in their church-going dress as they move from toddlers to teenagers. (These are Troyer Amish of Norwich, Ontario).

or is shifted to the back. A shoulder fastening is utilized by some women. In a number of groups the cape is sewn directly to the dress and shares its same back opening.

The Apron

There is evidence that western European women wore aprons as early as the 14th century.[3] Presently aprons are usually thought of as a protective, purely utilitarian garment. Such was not always the case. For the common woman an apron was an integral part of dress for both formal and informal occasions. While aprons have enjoyed periods of fashionable acceptance, only the common folk continued to wear them into the 19th century as part of their attire.

The apron, like the cape, has been regarded as an extra covering for the sake of modesty. Jacob Brubacher, a prominent Mennonite bishop of the 19th century is said to have made the statement, "The cape to cover the bosom, the apron to cover the abdomen. (Der Cape fer die Bruscht zudecke und der Shatz fer der Bauch zedecke.)"[4] While many of the more moderate plain women have dropped the apron but retained the cape, the Old Order woman very rarely appears in public without an apron.

Amish women of Berne, Indiana, follow an old custom of tying their apron strings in front. Note also the crossover black cape on the oldest girl and the black pinafore aprons of the younger girls.

This picture clearly illustrates the type of garb worn by Old Colony Mennonites in Mexico.

Aprons are of several different types. The waistband apron may be worn for dress occasions or for work. The oldest type has long strings which are crossed in the back and tied in front. These are seen among some Amish and Hutterites. In many groups the work apron is tied in the back, while the dress apron is pinned, snapped, hooked or buttoned at the side. In a few cases the apron is sewn or zippered to the dress. (The Old German Baptists have it this way.)

The bib apron is a type of work apron with a flap in front that is either pinned to the dress or held up by straps. Among some Beachy Amish the bib apron may be made to match the dress and take the place of the two-piece cape and apron for daily wear. In very conservative groups the bib apron is not allowed at all.

A type of apron worn by young girls is called an "arm apron" because it has arm holes. It may also be called a "pinafore" or "front apron." This type has no waist band and covers the entire front of the dress. In the back, however, it is fastened only at the top, thus exposing the back of the dress. The arm apron is seen most often among the more traditional groups.

The majority of plain women who wear the cape and apron make them of material which matches their dress. The more traditional

Old Orders have preserved the separate character of each garment by insisting that one or both be of a contrasting color from the dress. If all three pieces match, the combination is called a "suit" in some circles. White capes and/or aprons are part of the church-going dress in many Amish groups.

A conservative practice is to have the apron shorter than the dress to make it more apparent that an apron is being worn. Making the cape and apron of all one piece is considered more progressive.

The Short Gown

A two-piece style of dress, consisting of a bodice separate from the skirt in the form of a jacket, developed in the 15th century. This long-sleeved jacket varied in length but was usually considerably shorter than the skirt. In English it was known as a "short gown." This combination became typical of peasant garb over a wide area including America. Some black slaves of the early 19th century are pictured wearing this style.[5]

Many plain groups changed to a one-piece dress in the 19th century. The "Nebraska" or "white top" Amish, the Old Order River

Two types of headwear are shown on these Holmes County, Ohio, Amish women: the white head covering (cap) and the black bonnet which is worn over the head covering.

The two Old German Baptist women on the right wear bonnets and shawls. The woman on the left wears a sweater beneath the cape on her dress.

Brethren and the Reformed Mennonites have preserved the short-gown style. In most cases the bodice is now sewn to the skirt, but the characteristic peplum (often very reduced in size) remains. This is true of Lancaster County Amish. The Swartzentruber and Troyer Amish of the Midwest wear what is called a "yahk" dress (from the German word for jacket—"jacke"). In this case the bodice does not have a peplum but takes the form of a jacket worn over a sleeveless dress.

The Skirt

A long pleated or gathered skirt is common to most plain women. Some less traditional groups prefer gored skirts. A very old practice still observed by a few plain groups is to sew a tuck or fold around the lower part of the skirt. This feature, also seen in many peasant costumes, is to allow extra length to be added easily.

Plain churches have waged a constant battle against short skirts since their fashionable appearance in the 1920s. At that time there was a widespread rebellion in the Western world against traditional standards of decency and modesty. Fashionable hemlines rose rapidly from ankle to knee in less than a decade. Before this time, dress-length had hardly been an issue in plain churches, because society in general observed a very modest standard. Indeed there was a loud public outcry against the abbreviated "flapper" styles of the '20s from many sources and even proposed civil legislation in several states against the new short skirts.[6] This was all to no avail, however, and hemlines never returned to the lengths found in the centuries before World War I.

Women in non-tropical parts of the world had not traditionally worn dresses reaching much above the ankles until this time. One exception was certain isolated peasant costumes in mountain regions where long skirts were a hindrance in steep terrain. (Ironically, some plain groups may have come from such regions originally and may have worn short skirts when coming to America, but they soon changed to the accepted longer style.)[7]

Only a comparatively few plain groups have been successful in keeping the hemlines at the traditional ankle level. A common standard is midway between the ankle and knee or mid-calf length. As hemlines fluctuate with popular fashion, many plain women have followed to some extent. Strangely enough some plain women might be seen wearing dresses shorter than what is currently in style. This may be an expression of rebellion against church rules, or merely a measure of economy to wear out dresses that had once been stylish in length.

Mantles, Shawls, and Coats

One of the oldest garments to survive among plain people is the mantle or cloak. This outer wrap has been worn since very ancient times.[8] Currently this item is worn by adult women in only a few Amish groups in central and western Pennsylvania, but it is still a custom in many communities for very young girls to wear the mantle or "mandlie."

The mantle takes the form of a long tailored cape which is fastened up the front with buttons, snaps, or hooks. It usually has a wide, turnover collar, or it may have only a collar band at the neck. Slits for the arms in front may be present or absent.

The shawl largely replaced the mantle as an over-garment among the plain people. In the larger Western society, the shawl gained

These Swartzentruber Amish children from Ohio wear "mandlie" (mantles) and quilted bonnets. Very small Amish boys often wear some items of girls' clothing. (The child on the left is a boy, indicated by his pant legs.)

popularity in the early 1800s and is thought to be an adaption of an Oriental style. The shawl became the most typical outer wrap in the mid-19th century—the early Victorian era—symbolizing the propriety and respectability of this period.

The shawl is made of a large square piece of fabric, usually black wool. It is folded either into a triangle or rectangle, with fringe often present on its borders. The shawl is wrapped around the body and usually fastened with a large pin at the neck. The Old German Baptist Brethren have accepted a more tailored version of the shawl, which is actually more like a mantle.

Plain, full-length coats are preferred in many of the moderate groups. Old Order Amish and Mennonite women wear short coats for some occasions but not generally for church. In the more conservative groups a coat is not to be worn in public without a shawl over it. A plain dark coat is the typical everyday wrap of many Old Order women and especially school girls. The presence or absence of a turnover collar, lapels, outside pockets, and the method of fastening is subject to individual church regulations.

Many plain groups permit simple buttoned sweaters but not

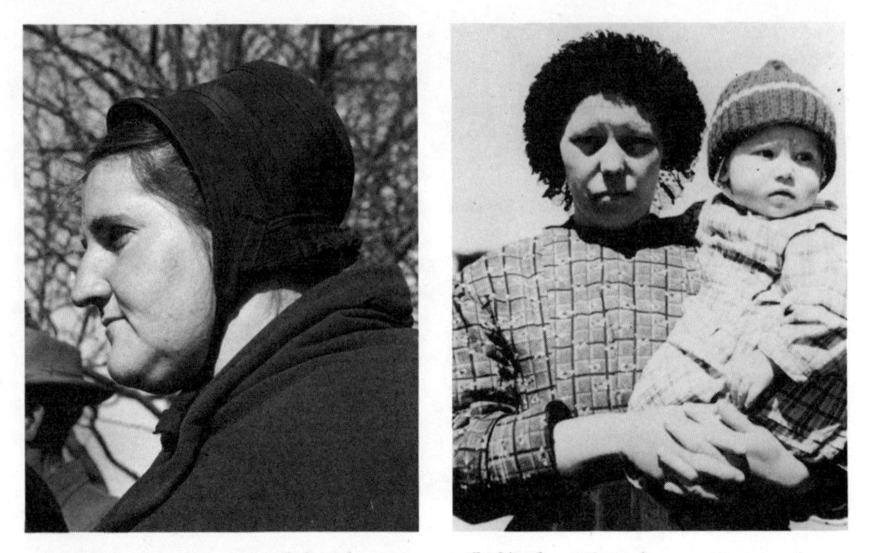

Two unique types of headwear are (left) the Victoria or Queen Anne bonnet of an Ontario Old Order Mennonite woman, and the "Mahtz," the headpiece of an Old Colony Mennonite from Mexico.

pullovers. Sweaters are forbidden in many Amish churches. In some places where they are allowed, they are to be worn only under a shawl or coat, and their buttons are often replaced with snaps or hooks. The objection to sweaters is probably based on their tendency to be form-fitting, and because they are usually obtained from the mass market and are, hence, subject to stylish fads. Since it is difficult to impose regulations on items such as sweaters that are not generally homemade or custom-made, they can become avenues of expression for fashionable desires.

Shoes

Shoes are another item that have not been made by the plain people themselves. For this reason there has been more change in shoe styles than in other areas of dress. In each generation an approved type of shoe comes to be recognized in each group. Since regulations on shoes are not as specific as those for other clothing, liberties are often taken in choosing more stylish types.

During the last half of the 19th century, high-topped shoes replaced the slipper-type shoes worn previously. Probably since this change was in the direction of greater modesty, plain women soon accepted them. When women's high-top shoes went back out of favor in the 1920s, some Amish and Hutterite groups retained the old style. Among the Swartzentruber and Troyer Amish, high shoes are worn in the cold season and low shoes in the warm season. Many conservative churches, especially the Amish, require that shoes be of the laced type.

Quite often black is the only accepted color for shoes. Sneakers and other canvas styles are rejected as too sporty by some churches, but many Old Orders do wear them. Sandals are approved for everyday wear in some groups, but the more traditional groups see them as a contemporary fad rather than a reversion to a biblical mode.

Stockings

The type of stockings women were to wear did not become an issue among plain people until the 20th century. Before that time, women's stockings were simply not seen in public. Black stockings were by far the most common type before the 1920s. But hosiery became increasingly thinner as hemlines rose, and finally, sheer,

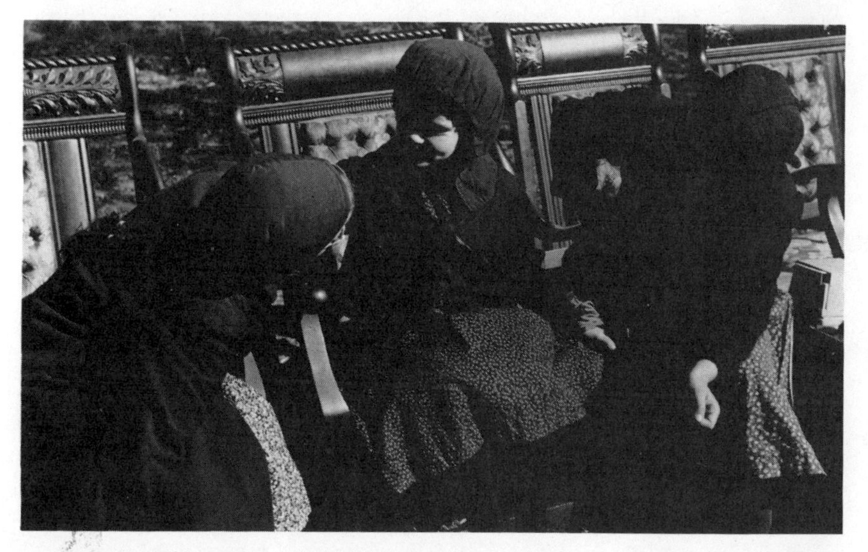

Ontario Old Order Mennonite girls wear heavy caps (shown) in cold weather and sunbonnets in warm weather.

flesh-colored stockings came into vogue to more effectively display the now exposed lower limbs.

While many plain people did eventually fall in line with the fashionable shorter skirts, they did not give up black stockings as quickly. Since the fight to keep the hemline near the ankle was largely lost, black stockings were probably seen to at least provide a degree of modesty. The tendency for stockings to become thinner and thinner has sometimes been met with rules specifying the deniers, the weight of material to be used.

Virtually all Old Orders and many of the more moderate groups require women to wear black stockings. For many informal occasions, plain women might wear neither shoes nor stockings. Amish children often go barefooted to school and church in warm weather, and it is not unknown for adults to do so in some communities.

Pantyhose are frequently worn by modern plain women. However this new item of apparel does present a problem when the ritual of feet washing is observed. Among Old German Baptist Brethren, the seams at the toes are taken out and the hose are rolled back for the occasion. Most simply wear some other kind of leg-wear on those days.

The woman in the middle wears a quilted winter bonnet; the other three women wear lightweight summer bonnets. (Swartzentruber Amish—Ohio)

The Bonnet

The black bonnet has become somewhat the symbol of the plain woman. It seems to best put into practice the "shamefacedness" spoken of in the Bible. The bonnet worn for outdoor weather protection is not to be confused with the cap or prayer covering worn under the bonnet.

The origin of the plain bonnet is rather obscure. While small, fashionable bonnets made their appearance at the turn of the 18th century, simple black bonnets were worn by English country women a few decades earlier. Their unfashionableness is verified by a statement made in the 1780s, describing something that was, "as unsuitable as linsey-woolsey or a black bonnet at the opera."[9]

Before the characteristic scoop bonnet was introduced to American Quakers at the very close of the 18th century, another type bonnet, called the wagon bonnet, was found on some Quaker women. It received its name from its shape which resembled the top of a covered wagon. A long curtain or bavolet around the edge of the wagon bonnet extended over the shoulders (a feature not seen on fashionable bonnets until nearly 50 years later). The wagon bonnet looked very much like a present day Amish bonnet.[10]

Popular bonnets of the 1840s were very similar in appearance to present plain bonnets. These were called "poke" bonnets or "coal scuttle" bonnets. When wearing one of these, a woman's face could not be seen except from directly in front. Fashion historians describe the 1840s as a time of extreme prudery, severity, and modesty.[11] It is said to have been the most fashionably static and stereotyped decade in the 19th century.[12] All of these criticisms would have been considered virtues by the plain people. It is no wonder that they have felt justified in adopting some of the outward characteristics of this age. Whether the plain bonnet was an adaption of the wagon bonnet of the late 18th century or the poke bonnet of the mid-19th century, cannot be determined at this late date. The latter could have very well been a carry-over of the former.

Fashionable bonnets became increasingly smaller in the latter part of the 19th century and by the 1880s were abandoned altogether. Some groups of plain women made certain modifications in their bonnet down through the years, while others have retained the very large traditional bonnets up to the present day.

The bonnet brim has been constructed of various materials including cardboard, either in a single piece or in long narrow slats sewn in individually (these are still used by Somerset County Pennsylvania Amish). Celluloid and door screen are also used for bonnet brims and, recently, cut-down plastic bleach bottles have been utilized for this purpose. Buckram is a common material for both bonnet brims and crowns. Metal wire is often used for reinforcement and shaping the bonnets.

Heavily quilted bonnets are worn in the winter in several Old Order groups. Felt crowns are typical of some smaller bonnets. Lightweight and often light-colored sunbonnets are worn for outdoor work in some Mennonite and Hutterite groups.

Some groups have cut back the bonnet brim away from the face and either greatly reduced or eliminated the curtain or bavolet at the neck. Among some Mennonites in the East, the bonnet has shrunk to a small "beanie" pinned to the back of the head, and even this is worn only by older women. Many of these beanie bonnets are now crocheted, often of colors other than the traditional black.

Long ribbons tied under the chin were the usual means of holding the bonnet on the head. A more recent Mennonite Church development was a chin-strap hooked at one side.

Many plain groups have dropped the wearing of bonnets altogether. This is usually one of the first items to go when a church departs from the Old Order. Various kinds of scarves or bandannas are worn for weather protection in the moderate groups. Even in groups where the bonnet is still required, a head scarf is often worn around the farm and on other informal occasions.[13]

Before the bonnet was accepted, plain and peasant women wore a wide-brimmed, shallow-crowned hat. This flat hat was made of felt or straw and was usually tied on with long ribbons. While this style did become popular in fashionable circles in the 18th century, its common name, "milkmaid hat," betrays its rural origin.

Some plain people were reluctant to replace the flat hats with bonnets, and one group, the "Nebraska" or "white top" Amish of central Pennsylvania, never did. In the Midwest some Amish women wear wide-brimmed straw hats similar or identical to men's hats for

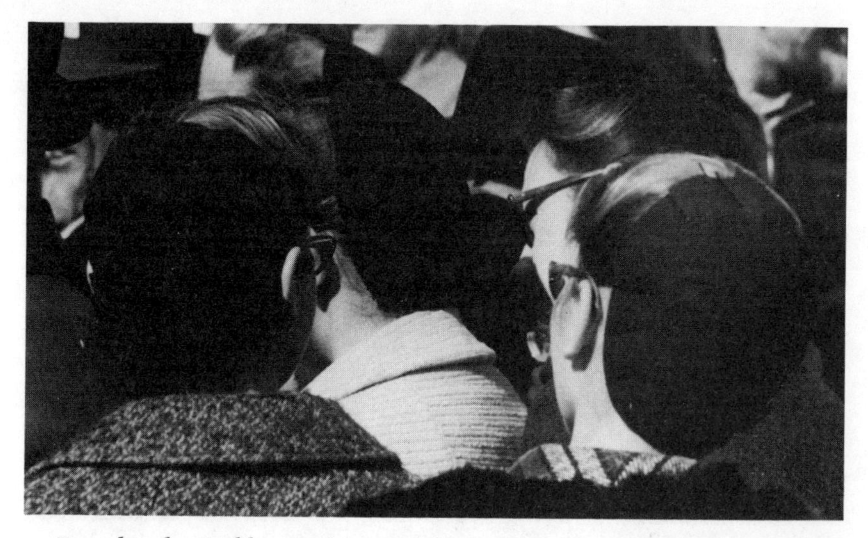

For church, Holdeman Mennonite women wear three-cornered black scarves tied beneath the chin. During the week many women fold the scarves into a beanie as shown here.

summer work occasions. Old Colony Mennonite women adopted a distinctive wide straw hat after their move to Mexico.

The Cap or Covering

A plain woman is seldom seen in public without some kind of covering on her head. This practice was very widespread in Western society from ancient times until the late 19th century. Customs varied as to who, where, and what kind of headdress was worn. A cap was sometimes looked upon as a symbol of marriage. In some churches coverings were worn by women only for the worship experience, a practice upheld by the Catholic church until quite recently. The early church fathers had established this custom in the first centuries of Christianity. John Calvin was very firm in his belief that a woman's head should be covered.[14] The Shaker foundress, Ann Lee, remarked to an early seeker, "Being a daughter of Zion, how camest thou hither without a cap on thy head?"[15]

When women largely discarded the wearing of caps after 1840, the plain people became staunch defenders of this time-honored practice. It is difficult to know how much religious significance the

Distinctive features of these Lancaster County, Pennsylvania, Amish girls' dress are the heart-shaped head coverings with a single pleat down the back, wide necklines, black aprons, wide apron belts, and small "leppli" (tabs) at the back of the waistlines.

head covering had to plain people before this time. Some very conservative plain people regard the cap as an essential part of a woman's dress but do not fully base the practice on Scriptural teaching. Others point to the Bible to explain why they both advocate and wear it.

The Scripture passage in I Corinthians 11:1-16, is given as the proof text for the observance of the woman's head covering. It is believed that these verses teach that a woman's head should be covered in symbolic obedience to God's order of creation: God-Christ-man-woman. It is to be worn when "praying or prophesying," so it is often called a prayer covering or prayer veiling. Many women feel it is so important that they wear some form of covering even in bed.

Unlike some other conservative Christians, the plain people believe this chapter teaches there are to be two coverings: the woman's natural long hair plus something placed over the hair. The plain people feel that the Apostle Paul was not only speaking to a peculiar situation in the Corinthian church but to Christians of all times in all lands. Conservative plain churches put the head covering on the equal basis with the doctrines of communion and baptism.

The form of covering varies from group to group but most often takes the form of a simple cap, usually white but sometimes black. Materials range from opaque muslin to very sheer net. The oldest type is made with a crown and a front piece that often extends over the ears. Tie strings, whether actually used to hold on the cap or not, are the mark of a conservative group. Some white Mennonite caps have black tie strings. Some insist that if strings are present the cap will tend not to get too small. Coverings are often pinned to the hair, but some women do actually tie them tightly under the chin.

Groups of Russian Mennonite background, which still practice the wearing of a head covering, make use of three-cornered kerchiefs or large head shawls. Many plain women who wear a cap for formal occasions replace it with a scarf or handkerchief around home. In many Mennonite and Brethren churches, a covering is not worn by girls until they experience conversion or have attained church membership. In some Amish communities and among Old Order Mennonites, girls wear a cap only at church services until adolescence when they begin wearing it all the time. In many

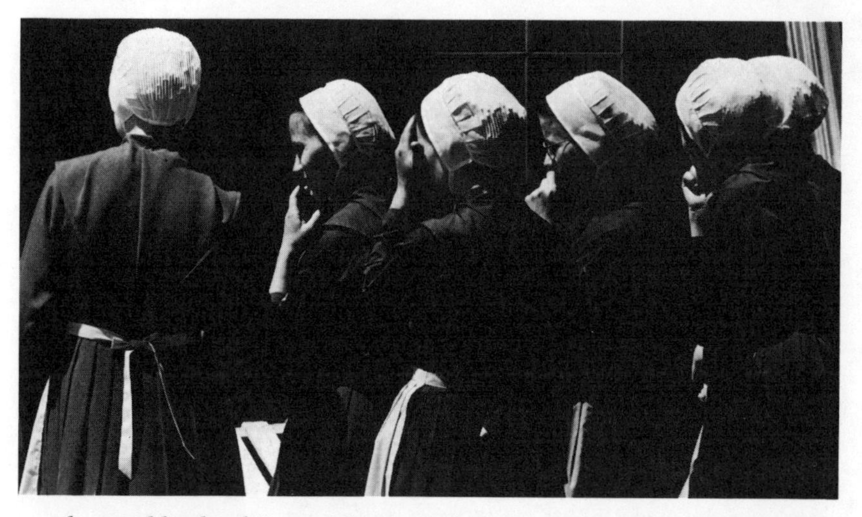

These Ashland, Ohio, Amish women have many fine pleats on the crowns of their head coverings and a small bow at the back of their necks. Some of the women wear light-colored work aprons.

Mennonite and Brethren churches women do not wear a covering except in worship services. This has been true for many years in a number of locations. It was the custom in some areas to keep caps stored in special boxes in the anterooms of the meetinghouses. Nowadays the coverings of marginal plain people are often carried to and from church in the wearer's purse.

In many churches the covering has been reduced to a very small, net skullcap. It may have lace edging or be made entirely of a lacy material. In these cases it is usually the only distinctive item of dress worn by a woman. The covering is usually the last vestige of plainness to survive. These covering-wearers do not see the cap as one part of a total way of dress, but as the carrying out of a specific biblical command. One will occasionally see a woman in slacks wearing a covering.

A Woman's Hair

In I Corinthians 11, the same chapter in the New Testament that refers to the head covering, it is also stated that, "If a woman have long hair it is a glory to her" (verse 15). The shamefulness of a woman being "shorn or shaven" is also spoken of. Most plain

Plain women believe the Bible teaches in 1 Corinthians 11 that they are not to cut their hair. These Lancaster, Pennsylvania, Amish girls show how the hair is typically arranged in a bun.

Amish girls in the Milverton, Ontario, community wear their hair in uniquely arranged braids.

Christians interpret this to mean that women's hair should be uncut. In conservative churches women always wear their hair pinned up in knots or buns which are concealed by their coverings. It is thought that a woman's "glory" is not for the whole world to see but is reserved for her husband alone.

In most Old Order groups, the girls' hair is worn up at a very early age. In some groups a young girl will wear her hair in long braids. This is not thought to conflict with the injunction against braided or plaited hair spoken of in the epistles, which is instead interpreted to mean very elaborate coiffures and not simple pigtails.

In most plain groups the women part their hair in the center of their heads. Much admonition is give against showing pride in one's hair. Despite these efforts, hair is often waved, curled, fluffed, and combed far down on the forehead. The covering and bonnet may be slid back to reveal a female's carefully arranged tresses.

12. Men's Clothing

The Hat

A broad-brimmed hat has been the symbol of the devout believer in the Judeo-Christian world for many centuries. Its use by such diverse groups as Catholic clergymen, Hasidic Jews, and nearly all groups of plain people attest to its widespread religious symbolism. The broad brim's ascetic appeal no doubt comes from its functional simplicity—a hat merely to provide shade and protection.

Anabaptists were distinguished by their broad felt hats at the very onset of the movement in the 1520s,[1] long before broad brims became popular in the mid 1600s. Quakers, Shakers, and Brethren have all adopted the plain hat as an important part of their dress.

The width of the brim and hat band and the height and shape of the crown are variables which gauge the orthodoxy of the group and individual wearer. A wide brim, low crown, and narrow hat band denotes the oldest, most traditional style. Within church groups one's age and status is often reflected by the dimensions of one's hat.

For warm weather, straw hats are preferred by plain men. Most of these are purchased in dry goods stores, but the Lancaster, "Nebraska," and Swartzentruber Amish produce their own hats made from strips of braided straw.

Caps with bills are discouraged in most Old Order churches. In moderate groups a bill cap is worn during the week and a brimmed plain hat for church and other formal occasions. Stocking caps are

The broad-brimmed hat has been a distinctive symbol of plain men for centuries. (Swartzentruber Amish)

Lehrerleut Hutterites, Saskatchewan (Note the distinctive cap of the boy).

very popular in many Old Order Amish communities, but these would never be worn to church.

Hair

There was a time when Old Order Amish men were criticized for having long hair. Later their hair was considered comparatively short, but the Amish hairstyle has varied very little. As with other matters of personal appearance, the plain people have both sought to choose a hairstyle that best expresses their convictions, and then determined to stick with it no matter what the world around them does.

The Old Order Amish claim that combing the hair down in all directions from the crown is the natural way the hair grows. Some cut their hair in a "bowl" style; others prefer a "Dutch boy" cut with the bangs being shorter than the hair at the temples. The corner thus formed is thought to carry out the command in Leviticus which says the corners of the head should not be rounded. Other plain people think this rounding refers to the shingling of the hair on the back of the head. Their hair is blocked (cut straight off in back) or "polled," to use a biblical term. Using a center part or combing the hair straight back is seen as an expression of nonconformity among conservative Brethren groups.

The more moderate plain groups, especially Mennonites, adopted the closely cropped style with a side part that gained popularity in the mainstream society late in the 19th century. By the early 1900s, the severely tapered cut was virtually the universal hair style of the Western man and continued to be so until the 1960s. When the Beatles came along with their mop tops and irreverent behavior, a reaction took place that established the standard man's haircut of the first part of the century as the symbol of the "clean cut" (and hence Christian) man. This style was also sanctioned by the scriptural injunction that "it is a shame for a man to have long hair."

The Beard

The Amish, Brethren, and Hutterites have always encouraged or required men to wear the beard. The Mennonites, Quakers, and Shakers have fluctuated on this issue. Some groups regard the beard as merely a symbol of nonconformity. In some cases it is the mark of a married man. One group does not require the beard until

Lancaster, Pennsylvania, Old Order Amish (In this community buttons are permitted on everyday work coats).

the first child is born. Others feel that God created man with a beard and it is an act of rebellion to cut it off. The beard is thought of as a natural means of sex distinction. The prophecy concerning Christ which says, "I gave my cheeks to them that plucked off the hair,"[2] is given as a text to prove Jesus wore a beard.

Many plain men do not trim the ends of the beard because of the command in Leviticus, "Neither shalt thou mar the corners of the beard."[3] Traditionally, most beard-wearing plain churches have observed shaving off the mustache. It is thought that this practice originated as an effort to abstain from the evil appearance of European soldiers with their curled mustachios. Some feel the mustache is unclean.

There is an increasing movement in many plain circles toward wearing the mustache with the beard. Virtually no plain church permits the mustache to be worn without the beard. This is thought to be purely an expression of worldliness. The plain people who wear the mustache with the beard feel it is a rightful part of the rest of the beard.

Most groups of conservative Mennonites do not promote the wearing of beards. (Old Order Mennonite—Ontario)

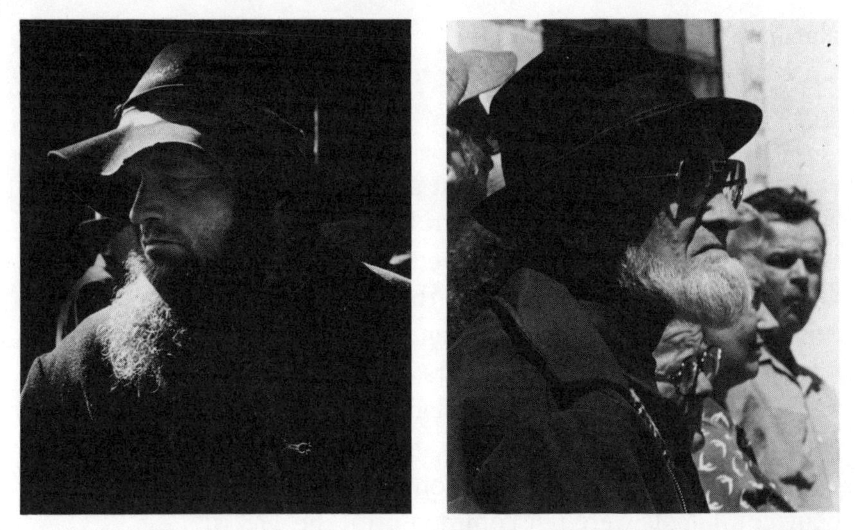

Hooks and eyes are clearly visible on the Ontario Amish man's coat (left). The man on the right is typical of the older generation of Beachy Amish.

Various ways of trimming the beard are observed among the plain groups. Some do not trim at all, while other have little more than a constant five-o'clock shadow or a few bristles on the chin. A Beachy Amish church warns in its standards, "Married men should wear beards that do not convey an apologetic message."

A number of conservative Mennonite groups are strongly opposed to the beard. Some say the beard is the mark of fallen man after Adam's sin. Another argument is that while the beard does grow naturally, man in his natural state is not pleasing to God. Some have tried to prove that Christ did not wear a beard. Many Mennonites have not wished to identify with the modern hippy movement (or, for that matter, with other plain people whom they consider to be lacking spiritually). In the minds of many Mennonites, the growing of a beard would simply be a departure from a long established practice and thus would tend to elevate or alienate a man from his brethren.

Some rather heated discussions have centered on the beard. One time a smooth-faced, plain man was approached by a beard-wearer on the ethics of shaving. The scorching reply was, "I don't want to look like an old dog dragging around a dead ground hog!" On another occasion the statement was made, "Half the sincere Christians I know don't have beards . . . they're women."

The Coat

The practice of wearing a coat as part of a man's suit began in the 1660s.[4] Coats had been worn before this by some men of the working class and also as overcoats, but the most common fashionable upper garment was the doublet (a short, tight jacket originally designed as padding beneath armor).[5] The first suit coats were knee-length, had no collars or lapels, and buttoned to the neck. Standing and turnover collars appeared in the 18th century, and, beginning about the 1740s, the skirts of the coats gradually began to curve away from the stomach to form the so-called shad-belly cut. Lapels were not common until the 1780s.[6]

The coat with a standing collar and split tail adopted by plain men was similar to the mid-18th century style. Unlike fashionable examples of this period, plain coats did not have extra ornamental buttons, and several sources indicate the typical pockets with flaps were absent.[7] Toward the end of the century some stylish coats did

(Left) William U. Ditzler (1821-1897) and (right) Samuel Morris (1827-1905), members of the Society of Friends, wear the distinctive style of Quaker plain coat.

A group of Old German Baptist Brethren men wear plain frock coats and plain black hats.

not have outer pockets, but these usually had a turnover collar.[8]

A study of costume histories and contemporary portraits reveals that the standing collar was very rare among the general population after 1800. In the 19th century the standing collar was seen only on a few traditional ceremonial coats, some types of uniforms, the informal street wear of many clergymen, and, of course, among the various plain groups. The functional simplicity of this style no doubt accounts for its acceptance in such diverse groups.

The German Baptist Brethren (Dunkers) tried to establish at their 1877 Annual Meeting which style of coat was most ancient to their group. The moderator, Daniel P. Saylor (1811-1885) of Beaverdam, Maryland, stated that he, his father (1775-1850), and grandfather (1753-1840) all wore the standing collar coat and knew of no other tradition among the Brethren.[10]

The Mennonites who came from Bern, Switzerland, to Berne, Indiana, in the 1850s wore the standing collar coat.[11] A minister from this group, Samuel Sprunger (1848-1923), is shown wearing such a coat in the Wadsworth Institute class picture of ca. 1868-1869.[12] There are many English and American drawings showing early 1800s Quaker men wearing the plain coat and mid-1800s

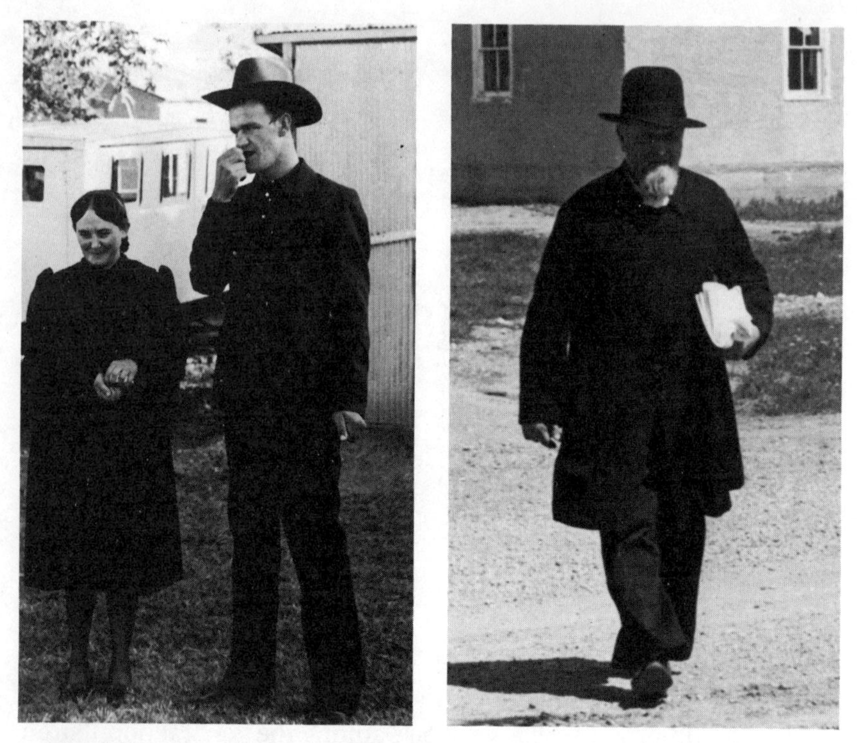

The Old Colony Mennonite man (left) wears a conventional sack coat with a black shirt and no tie. A long frock coat is worn by a Hutterite minister, (right).

photographs of Quaker, Mennonite, and Amish men also clearly wearing this style.[13]

Among the plain people the plain coat has been modified in various ways. Many traditional groups rounded off the corners of the neckline; others preferred a notch or step in the collar in front. Some who wanted to appear more stylish turned back the corners at the neck to form lapels (although retaining the standing collar). After 1900 the shad-belly cut was replaced in many groups by a style that fastened all the way down the front.[14]

During most of the 18th and 19th centuries, the pattern for virtually all men's coats featured a split tail and seams curving down from the arm junctures in back. This seems somewhat elaborate today, but apparently no one considered making a coat in any other way for nearly 200 years. This style with a standing collar became known as the plain frock coat or "mutze" among the plain people. Nearly all Old Order plain men wear this kind of coat for church and other formal occasions.

The short, loose-fitting sack coat (the conventional suit coat of today) gradually gained popularity among the fashionable after 1840,[15] and eventually replaced other styles except those used for some very formal occasions. About 1900, among some plain groups, standing collars were put on sack coats to form a new kind of plain coat. Among non-Old Order groups of conservative Mennonite and Brethren men, this became the most common style by the 1930s. Unlike the plain frock coat, the plain sack coat usually had outside pockets, typically three. Among Lancaster and Franconia Conference Mennonites, the plain frock coat continued to be required of the ministry until the 1960s. In these groups the plain sack coat was worn by a large percentage of lay members. In many Amish communities sack coats (wamus) without outer pockets are worn by men for non-church occasions, while non-member boys wear this type for church as well.

Among Mennonites the plain coat has also been known as the straight-cut coat or officially as the regulation coat. In groups where this style is only encouraged rather than required, it has been derisively known as a chin-cutter or choke-coat by those who do not wear it.

Some plain groups did not retain the standing collar coat, and conventional coats with turnover collars became the norm. The progressive Amish Mennonites who broke with the Old Order in the late 1800s accepted lapel coats but at first required that they have hooks and eyes. In the Conservative Mennonite Conference (of Amish Mennonite origin) many men wear lapel coats without ties. This is also becoming increasingly common in some other Mennonite groups among men who had once worn the plain coat. In many of the more conservative Mennonite groups, conventional lapel coats are worn by boys until conversion or church membership. In most Old Order Mennonite groups a plain coat is not worn until after marriage. Old Colony Mennonite ministers wear long frock coats with lapels and turnover collars, while other men wear conventional sack coats without neckties.

Pants

One might assume that the transition from knee breeches to long trousers among tradition-oriented plain people caused quite a controversy. There is no evidence that this was the case. Breeches replaced a variety of different kinds of leg wear being worn in the 16th century, such as the pumpkin-shaped shorts known as trunk hose. There is plenty of evidence that plain men wore knee breeches in the 17th and 18th centuries. But before trousers became fashionable in about 1800, they were worn by farmers, sailors, and other commoners.[16]

It is probable that some plain men accepted this mode at an early date since it was the mark of a common man. Samuel Johnson's 1754 *Dictionary* defines "galligaskins" as "loose fitting Anabaptist trousers." The Franconia Mennonite alms book records that long trousers were made for a needy man in 1772.[17] Few plain people retained knee breeches beyond 1850.[18] It was probably obvious that long trousers presented a more modest appearance.

When fly closures for pants were introduced in the 1820s, some considered them indecent. In 1830 the *Gentleman's Magazine of Fashion* pronounced the fly, "an indelicate and disgusting fashion." While the larger society eventually accepted this feature, many plain people did not. For much of the 18th century a flap or fall was provided on the front of men's trousers or breeches (as on European lederhosen). This was usually rather narrow and fastened with two or three buttons. An alternate and more easily made type had the flap all the way across the front. This was called the broadfall. It was this type that was adopted by most Old Order plain men.

No plain group currently uses the narrow fall, although it was known among Old Order River Brethren in the early part of the 20th century. Sailor pants also had the broadfall, but unlike the plain version, it buttoned up the sides as well as across the top (plain broad falls usually have four buttons on the flap while navy pants have 13).

Some recent innovations, such as creases down the pant legs, hip pockets, and cuffs, have been prohibited among many groups of plain people, notably the Amish. Bell-bottoms and tight, form-fitting pants have also met with disapproval.

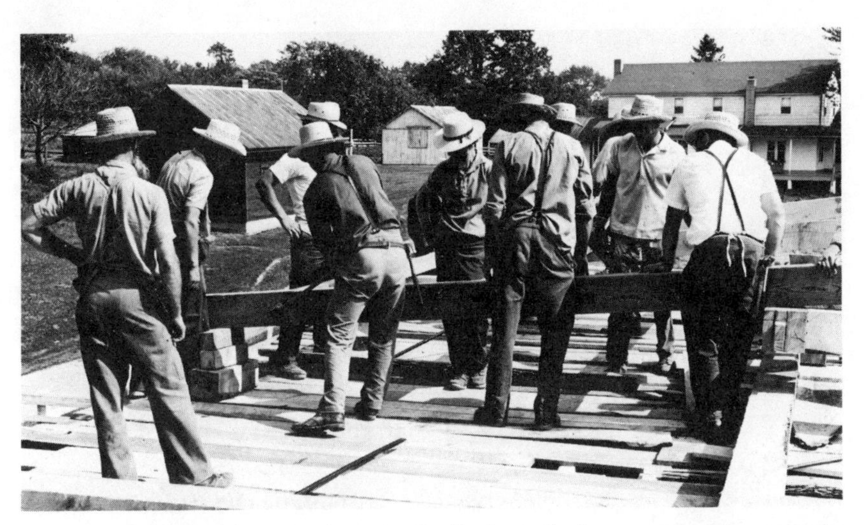

Several kinds of suspenders (or lack thereof), hats, and shirts can be observed in this group of Holmes—Wayne County, Ohio, Amish men. There are several separate groups of Amish in this community.

Suspenders

A colonial man's pants were held up by laces at the back of the waistband. Suspenders were introduced in the late 1700s.[19] At first many plain people objected to suspenders, but later most groups did accept them. The "Nebraska" Amish have preserved the old style laced pants. Eventually suspenders came to symbolize rural old-fashionedness, an image plain people could readily identify with. Conservative groups of Amish, Mennonites, Brethren, and Hutterites have all made suspenders an integral part of men's dress. Some Amish groups did not accept suspenders without some modification. The Renno and Byler Amish of Pennsylvania allow only one strap which is worn diagonally across the right shoulder. The Swartzentruber and Troyer Amish require that the straps form a "Y" in the back rather than the usual "X." Others do not allow elastic, metal, or buckles.

In the 1890s belts were only beginning to be worn as a part of men's everyday attire. Mail-order catalogs of this period indicate that belts were primarily worn only for sports such as tennis, basketball, and bicycling. The 1897 Sears catalog tried to convince

Unlike other Old Order plain people, many Ontario Old Order Mennonite youth wear caps and long neckties.

men that belts were popular and were being worn by "all classes of people." The plain people possibly resisted wearing belts because of their associated sporty appearance, which would have been very much opposed to their emphasis on sobriety.

Belts are found among some moderate groups of plain people. In certain instances, such as some Beachy Amish and Old German Baptist Brethren, belts are worn with broadfall pants.

The Shirt

Originally the shirt was considered an item of underwear. Indeed, for centuries it was often the only item of men's underwear. For this reason the shirt was never worn alone for formal occasions. This could be compared to a man wearing a T-shirt to church in the present age. Most Old Order plain people still believe that it is necessary to wear at least a vest over the shirt during the worship services. The "Swiss" Amish, those of Milverton, Ontario, and Canadian Old Order Mennonites require that a coat be worn for church even in the warmest weather.

One time an Old Order Mennonite bishop from the United States visited a Canadian congregation of his denomination. During the course of his sermon he removed his coat. This caused great alarm among the home ministry who insisted that even young boys keep their coats on during church.

The most traditional plain people have retained a "pullover" type shirt which opens only part-way down the front. The usual coat-type shirt of today did not become fashionably popular until the 20th century. The number of buttons, the type of collar, the width of the cuffs, and the presence of pockets are subject to local customs and church regulations. Many groups do not permit short sleeves, a trend that did not become popular in the world until the 1930s. Any kind of form-fitting knit shirts, T-shirts, or undershirts worn alone are forbidden in nearly all plain churches. Among conservative Mennonites, a long-sleeved shirt with the collar buttoned is considered a mark of nonconformity when the plain coat is not worn.

Among most Old Order Amish, white shirts are traditional for church. The "Nebraska" Amish wear white shirts for all occasions. With Ontario Old Order Mennonites, blue shirts are most traditional. Old Colony and Sommerfelder Mennonite ministers wear black shirts.

The Vest

Among Old Order Amish, Mennonites, and Brethren vests are an important item of attire. In Pennsylvania Dutch they are called jackets. Generally, the more conservative the group, the more often vests are worn. In some instances young boys even wear vests to school. Old Order Mennonites, Old Order River Brethren, and "Nebraska" Amish have a standing collar on their vests like is common on plain coats, but most groups have adopted the V-neck style. The Swartzentruber and Troyer Amish have preserved a style having three vents or splits in the back, a carry-over from a time when the vest was much longer.

The Necktie

Most plain groups feel very strongly that a necktie is a useless ornament. Some call it a piece of cloth jewelry. This conviction developed rather late in some of the large plain communities in the East. Some plain groups still feel that the tie is a proper part of man's dress. Bow ties are generally considered more conservative than a long tie. The common man's neckerchief may have been the origin of the plain man's tie rather than the cravats of the fashion-setters.[20]

The very conservative Reformed Mennonites continue to wear small black bow ties with their plain frock coats. Lancaster Old Order Amish and Old Order Mennonite boys had commonly worn bow ties, but the practice seems to be dying out. Among Ontario Old Order Mennonites long ties have long been approved, but here, too, ties are not as common as they had been.

Some Conservative Conference Mennonite congregations prohibit ties but do not require the plain coat. Here some men circumvent the ruling by wearing turtlenecks and stylish leisure jackets with an open-collared shirt.

Shoes

High laced shoes are the approved footwear in the more orthodox plain churches. The more moderate groups permit low shoes, but slip-on styles are generally held in disfavor. Black is the predominant color for dress shoes. Work shoes are often brown or tan.

Boots and high shoes became established as proper footwear in the Victorian era and later became the mark of a conservative or old-fashioned man. Again, this was sufficient reason for plain people to adopt this style as their own. Earlier in this century, short boots with elastic gussets were common among plain groups. Farmers wore short boots before riding boots become the rage around 1800.[21] In the 18th century low shoes were probably worn by plain people, but there is evidence that laces were specified in some groups rather than the prevalent buckles.[22] Rulings on shoes have been rather flexible since the plain people had to depend on mass-produced footwear. Only among the Hutterites have any plain groups endeavored to manufacture their own shoes.

Work Coats and Winter Coats

Whereas the dress coat is carefully regulated in most plain churches, the more moderate groups have had little to say about

The cape overcoat worn by the man at left is worn for some occasions in the most traditional Old Order groups. Short coats are worn more frequently.

everyday coats and jackets. The more conservative styles available in department stores are thought to be sufficiently plain in many churches. Those who do not wish to become dependent upon mass-produced apparel make their own everyday coats and jackets. Even in some of these groups a turnover collar is permitted on a work coat, whereas a standing collar is required on the dress coat.

The most conservative elements of each plain church family have preserved what was known as a "great coat" in the 18th century. This long, heavy overcoat has a large circular cape attached to the neckline which drapes down over the shoulders. There is also a small turnover collar. Some Old Order Amish and Mennonite churches expect the ordained man to wear this kind of coat while lay members are not required to do so. Very few automobile groups have kept the cape overcoat, and it has been abandoned by many horse and buggy churches. The acceptance of closed-front vehicles supposedly made the extra warmth of the cape unnecessary.

13.
Plain Dress in Detail

Plain people from diverse religious, cultural, national, and regional backgrounds have interpreted the principal of nonconformity in attire in various ways. Many basic elements of dress are shared by these different groups. However, there are multiple variations in the precise cut, color, and way of wearing which make each religious group and local community, within the larger religious groups, distinctive. The following brief descriptions and charts show some of the details observed by representative groups. It must be understood that some individuals within any church do not meet the minimum standards, while others go beyond what is required of them.

Practices observed by nearly all conservative plain people include women not cutting their hair and wearing it up on their heads, women not wearing makeup, jewelry, shorts, and slacks, and men not wearing shorts, a mustache without a beard, or going without a shirt. These are generally not mentioned in the group descriptions.

Old Order Amish

The accompanying drawings and charts demonstrate variations in practice in several of the older and larger Amish communities. There are a number of dress characteristics which apply to nearly all Amish (exceptions noted). These include the exclusive use of solid-colored fabrics and the forbiddance of wristwatches.

For men, hooks and eyes are used on suit coats and vests; hair is cut off straight in the back and worn in bangs in the front; adults wear long beards without a mustache; a hat is an integral part of daily dress; shirts have no pockets; broadfall pants without hip pockets are standard; a sack coat (wamus) is worn by boys for all dress-up occasions and by men for non-church dress-up; a frock coat (mütze) is obtained at baptism and is always worn for church thereafter; a minister must always wear a coat for church services, while other members must at least wear a vest; short work coats and winter coats are most typical; long overcoats with a cape are worn on some occasions by the more conservative; shoes are the laced type, high-tops being more conservative than oxfords.

For women, center-parted hair is worn in a bun (including small girls); caps (head coverings) have tie strings which are tied, at least for church, and daily by more conservative members; scarves and handkerchiefs are used in place of caps for daily wear by the less conservative; black caps are worn by singles, at least for church (customs vary a great deal as the chart shows); capes always have a point in the back; capes are always worn for church; in some areas they are worn daily while in other areas they are seldom worn for going away; aprons are always worn with dresses; aprons for "good" are often pinned on; work aprons usually tie in the back; the use of white capes and aprons for church is subject to various customs; pinafore aprons and dresses opening in the back (usually with buttons) are worn until adolescence; older girls' and womens' dresses are pinned or snapped up the front; black bonnets and shawls are the approved going-away outer wear; among the more conservative groups short coats may be worn only beneath shawls, but in less conservative areas short coats are worn alone; mantles are worn by adult women in a few very traditional areas and by small girls in many other places; black stockings and black, laced shoes are the general rule for going away, but bare feet are typical around home in warm weather.

Other Churches of Amish Background

Amish Mennonites

The Amish church divided into traditional and progressive camps in the last half of the 19th century. The progressives, called

Amish Women's Clothing

straight cape

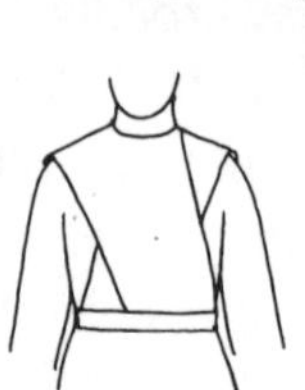
crossed cape

dress with "lappa"

Midwest (back)

Lancaster (back)

"Nebraska" (back)

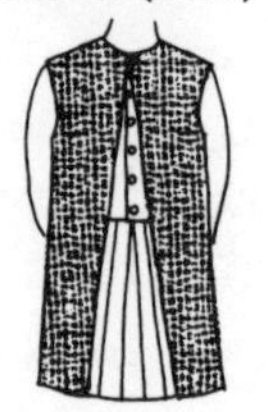
pinafore apron (back)

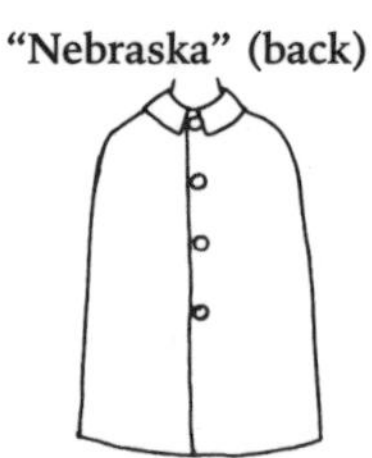
mantle (front)

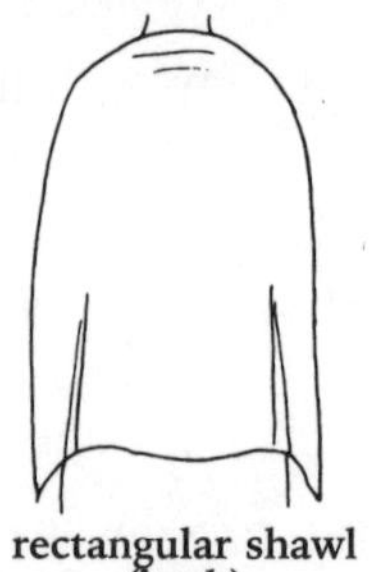
rectangular shawl (back)

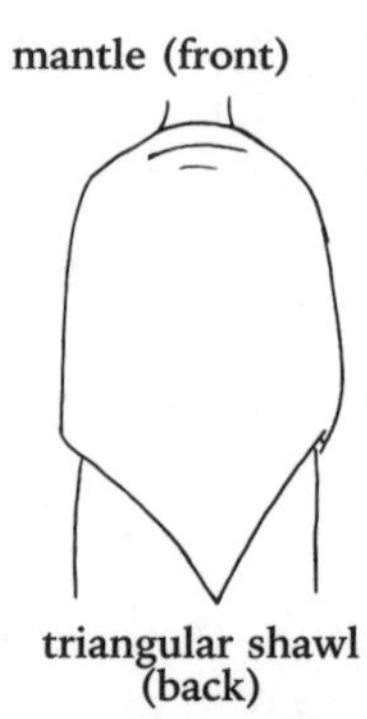
triangular shawl (back)

Community	Cap (head covering)	Cape	Apron
Lancaster Co., PA [1]	Single pleat, drawstring in back[2]	Straight	Pinned
Renno Group Mifflin Co., PA	Single pleat, drawstring in back	Crossed, always worn	Pinned
"Nebraska" Group Mifflin Co., PA	Multiple pleats, opaque material, drawstring in back, always tied	Crossed, always worn	Tied in front[9]
New Wilmington, PA	Multiple pleats, bow in back, always tied	Crossed, always worn	Tied in front
Somerset, Co., PA	Multiple pleats, bow in back	Straight, always worn, comes to point in front	Pinned
Dover, DE	Multiple pleats, bow in back	Straight	Pinned
Holmes Co., OH[13] (largest group)	Multiple fine pleats, bow in back	Crossed for unbaptized, straight for baptized	Pinned
Swartzentruber Group[14] Holmes-Wayne Cos., OH	Multiple pleats, bow in back, always tied	Crossed until 15, straight after 15, worn daily in cold months	Pinned
LaGrange Co., IN[16]	Multiple fine pleats, bow in back	Crossed	Pinned
Arthur, IL	Multiple elaborate pleats, bow in back	Crossed for single, straight for married	Pinned
Kalona, IA	Single pleat, bow in back	Crossed for single, straight for married	Pinned
Buchanan Co., IA[17]	Multiple pleats, bow in back	Crossed for single, straight for married	Pinned
Adams Co., IN[19]	No pleats	Crossed	Tied in front
Daviess Co., IN	Single pleat, bow in back	Straight	Pinned
Milverton, ON	Multiple pleats	Crossed, made from a square folded to a triangle	Pinned

* color matches dress color

** color contrasts with dress color

Dress	Girl's pinafore apron	Bonnet	Shawl	Mantle	At Church-Single	At Church-Married	Other Dress-Up Occasions-Single	Other Dress-Up Occasions-Married
Small peplum, pleated skirt[3]	To school, black, buttons or snaps	Stand-up crown, bow in back, various colors worn until 10	Rectangular	Rare, bright colors, until 3 or 4	White cape and apron, black cap (white cap in some districts)[4]	Matching or black cape, black apron, white cap[5]	Matching cape, black apron, white cap[6]	Matching or black cape, black apron, white cap[7]
Small peplum, pleated skirt	To school, matching* or black (sometimes other contrasting color)	Stand-up crown, bow in back, various colors until early grades in school	Rectangular	Worn before school-age	White cape and apron, black cap	Black cape and apron, white cap	Black (rarely matching) cape, black apron, white or black cap[8]	Black cape and apron, white cap
Large, wide peplum, pleated skirt, tucks on skirt[10]	Always worn, contrasting,** bow-fastening[11]	None worn; kerchief and flat hat instead[12]	None worn	Gray, worn by all ages	White cape and apron, black cap	White cape, contrasting apron, white cap	Contrasting cape and apron, white cap	Contrasting cape and apron, white cap
Small, wide peplum, pleated skirt, tucks on skirt	Always worn, matching or contrasting, bow-fastening	Brown, very simple	None worn	Black, worn by all ages	White cape and apron, black cap	White cape, matching or contrasting apron, white cap	Black or matching cape and apron, white or black cap	Black or matching cape and apron, white cap
Pleated skirt	To school, matching or contrasting	Slat-type, very large	Triangular	Until 6 or 7	White cape and apron, spring to fall; otherwise matching; black cap	Matching cape and apron, white cap	Matching cape and apron, black cap	Matching cape and apron, white cap
Pleated skirt	To school, matching	Midwest style	Triangular and rectangular	Until 7 to 9	White cape and apron, black cap	White cape, matching or white apron, white cap	Matching cape and apron, white or black cap	Matching cape and apron, white cap
Narrow lappa for church, pleated skirt	Often to school, matching	Midwest style	Rectangular for unbaptized, triangular for baptized	Sometimes worn on small girls	White cape and apron, black cap	White cape, matching or white apron, white cap	Matching cape and apron, white or black cap	Matching cape and apron, white cap
Jacket bodice with lappa, pleated skirt, tucks on skirt	Always worn, contrasting	Quilted for winter, white lining for summer	Triangular	Frequently worn by younger girls	White cape and apron, black cap	White cape, matching or white apron, white cap	Contrasting cape, matching apron, white or black cap[15]	Contrasting cape, matching apron, white cap
Mostly pleated skirt, some gathered	Often to school, matching	Midwest style	Rectangular	Sometimes worn on small girls	White cape and apron, black cap	White cape, matching or white apron, white cap	Matching cap and apron, white cap	Matching cape and apron, white cap
Mostly pleated skirt	Often to school, matching	Various colors until 4 to 6	Rectangular	Until 8 to 10	White cape and apron, black cap	White cape, matching or white apron, white cap	Matching cape and apron, white cap	Matching cape and apron, white cap
Gathered skirt	To school, matching, 3 or 4 buttons	Slat-type, bow in back	Rectangular	Rarely worn	White cape and apron, black cap	Matching cape and apron, white cap	Matching cape and apron, white cap	Matching cape and apron, white cap
Gathered skirt	To school, contrasting	Very large[18]	Rectangular	Until 6 to 8	White cape and apron, black cap	White cape, matching apron, white cap	Contrasting cape, matching apron, white or black cap	Contrasting cape, matching apron, white cap
Wide peplum, pleated skirt	To school, matching or contrasting	Midwest style	Rectangular or triangular	Until 12	White cape, matching or white apron, black cap	White cape, matching or white apron, black cap	Black cape, matching apron, black cap	Black cape, matching or black apron, black cap
Pleated or gathered skirt	Only to church, white	Midwest style	Rectangular	Until 8 or 9, only for church	Matching cape and apron, white cap	Matching cape and apron, white cap	Matching cape and apron, white cap	Matching cape and apron, white cap
Gathered skirt	To school, contrasting (light colors) until 13 or 14	Bow in back, not worn until 14	Triangular	Worn by small girls	Summer—white cape and apron; winter—white cape, black apron, black cap	Black cape and apron, white cap	Cape seldom worn, contrasting apron, black cap	Cape seldom worn, black apron, white cap

Amish Men's Clothing

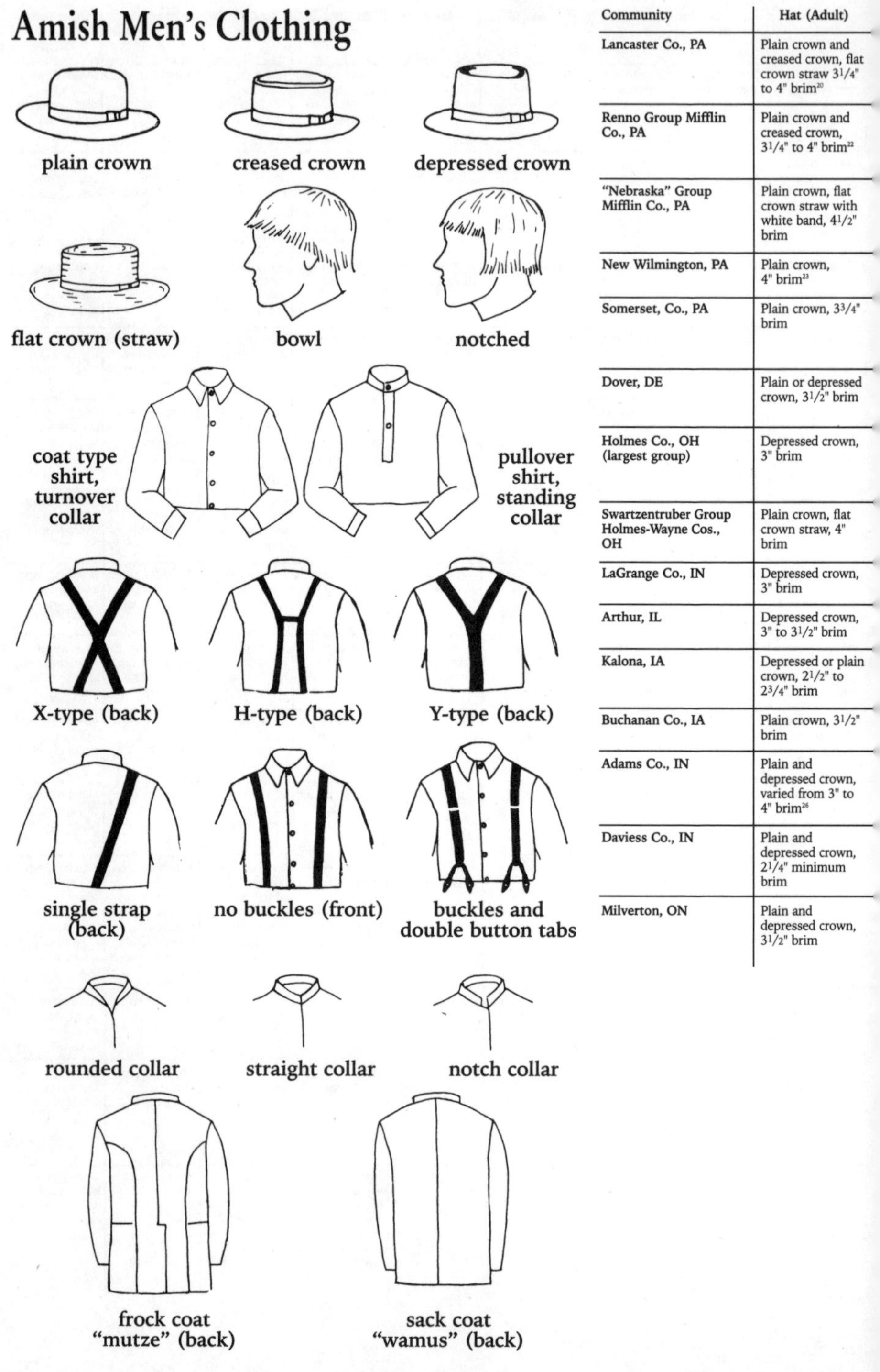

Community	Hat (Adult)
Lancaster Co., PA	Plain crown and creased crown, flat crown straw 3 1/4" to 4" brim[20]
Renno Group Mifflin Co., PA	Plain crown and creased crown, 3 1/4" to 4" brim[22]
"Nebraska" Group Mifflin Co., PA	Plain crown, flat crown straw with white band, 4 1/2" brim
New Wilmington, PA	Plain crown, 4" brim[23]
Somerset, Co., PA	Plain crown, 3 3/4" brim
Dover, DE	Plain or depressed crown, 3 1/2" brim
Holmes Co., OH (largest group)	Depressed crown, 3" brim
Swartzentruber Group Holmes-Wayne Cos., OH	Plain crown, flat crown straw, 4" brim
LaGrange Co., IN	Depressed crown, 3" brim
Arthur, IL	Depressed crown, 3" to 3 1/2" brim
Kalona, IA	Depressed or plain crown, 2 1/2" to 2 3/4" brim
Buchanan Co., IA	Plain crown, 3 1/2" brim
Adams Co., IN	Plain and depressed crown, varied from 3" to 4" brim[26]
Daviess Co., IN	Plain and depressed crown, 2 1/4" minimum brim
Milverton, ON	Plain and depressed crown, 3 1/2" brim

Hair	Beard	Shirt	Suspenders	Frock coat	Work coat	Cape overcoat
Notched, medium length	After marriage	Turnover collar; old—pullover, 4 buttons; new—coat-type	X-type, elastic; old—no buckles; new—buckles	Rounded collar[21]	Buttons; old—standing collar; new—turnover collar	Required of ministry
Notched, medium length	At baptism	Turnover collar; old—pullover, 3 buttons; new coat-type	1 strap, elastic	Rounded collar	Hooks, standing collar	Worn by most older men but few young
Notched, very long	Before baptism	Turnover collar, pullover, 2 buttons, white only	None, pants laced up in back	Rounded collar	Hooks, standing collar	Commonly worn, no outside pockets
Notched, long	At baptism	Standing collar, pullover, 3 buttons	None[24]	Rounded collar	Hooks, standing collar	Commonly worn
Bowl, medium length	About one year after baptism	Standing collar, usually 4 buttons	X-type, elastic, buckles	Notch collar	Hooks, standing collar	Mostly worn by ministers, long overcoat without cape worn by others
Bowl, medium length	After baptism, before first communion	Standing collar, pullover, usually 4 buttons	X-type, elastic, no buckles	Straight collar	Snaps, standing collar	Rare
Bowl, medium length	At baptism	Old—standing collar, pullover, 3 buttons; new—turnover collar, coat-type	None or X-or H-type, non-elastic, no buckles	Straight collar	Hooks or snaps, standing or turnover collar	Rare
Notched, long	At baptism	Standing collar, pullover, 2 buttons	Y-type, non-elastic, no buckles	Rounded collar	Hooks, standing collar	Commonly worn
Bowl, medium length	At marriage	Turnover collar, coat-type	None or X-type, elastic, no buckles	Notch collar	Snaps, turnover collar	Rare
Bowl, medium length	At marriage	Turnover collar, coat-type	None or X-type, elastic, no buckles	Notch collar	Hooks or snaps, turnover collar	Rare
Bowl, medium to short, center part	At marriage	Turnover collar,[25] coat-type, pockets allowed	X-type, elastic, buckles	Notch collar	Hooks or snaps	Rare, long overcoat without cape worn
Bowl, medium to long	At baptism	Standing collar, pullover, 3 buttons	X-type, elastic, no buckles	Straight collar	Hooks, standing collar	Commonly worn
Bowl, medium length	At baptism	Turnover collar, pullover or coat-type, hooks or snaps	X-type, elastic, buckles	Rounded collar	Hooks, standing or turnover collar	Commonly worn
Bowl, medium to short	At marriage	Turnover collar, 2 buttons and snaps, coat-type	X-type, elastic, buckles	Notch collar	Hooks or snaps, turnover collar	Rare
Bowl, medium to short	At marriage	Turnover collar, 2 buttons[27]	X-type, elastic, buckles	Rounded neckline (no collar)	Hooks, turnover collar	Required of ministry

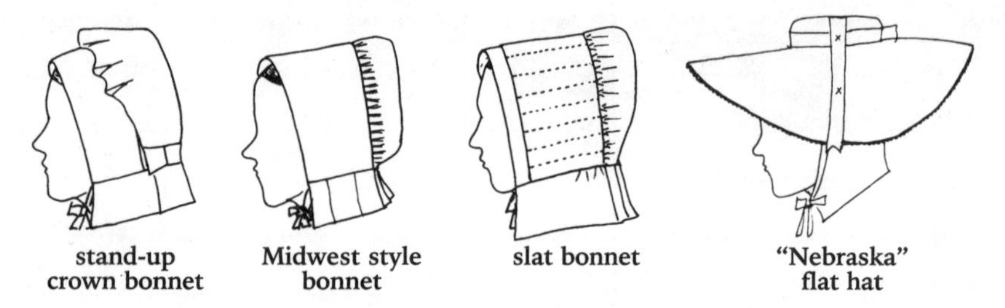

stand-up crown bonnet — Midwest style bonnet — slat bonnet — "Nebraska" flat hat

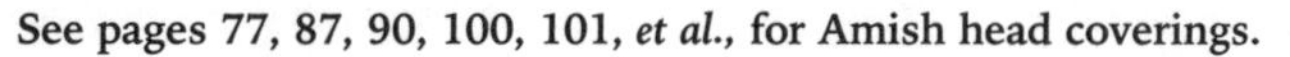
See pages 77, 87, 90, 100, 101, *et al.*, for Amish head coverings.

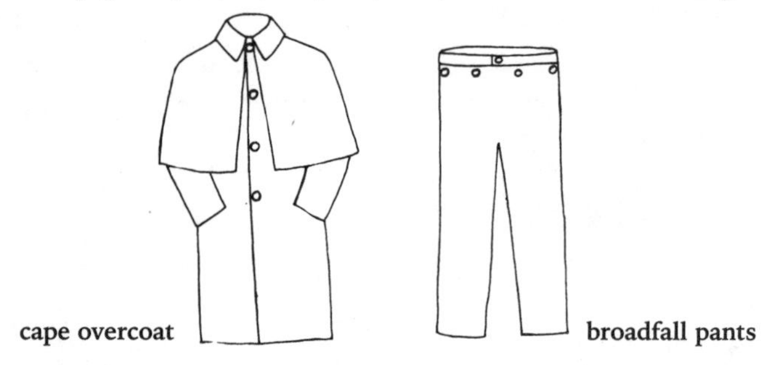

cape overcoat — broadfall pants

Amish Mennonites, merged with the Mennonite Church in the period 1917-1927. Amish dress characteristics (beards, hooks and eyes, etc.) vanished very rapidly among these people after 1900. Plain coats and cape dresses were never widely accepted among Amish Mennonites; however, many men did not wear neckties. Most Mennonite churches of Amish Mennonite background have largely dropped all distinctive dress, including women's head coverings.

Conservative Mennonite Conference *(organized 1910)* and Western Ontario Mennonite Conference *(organized 1922)*

These conferences were formed by independent Amish churches which were midway between the Amish Mennonites and the Old Order Amish in their practices. Since 1950 they have become more like the Mennonite Church. A few churches do not allow wedding bands or neckties and require women to wear their uncut hair pinned up and require the daily wearing of the head covering.

Many of the more conservative churches in these groups withdrew to form "non-conference" congregations and fellowships in the 1950s and '60s.

Kauffman Amish Mennonite *(Sleeping Preacher Amish)*

This group is a result of a movement led by John D. Kauffman among Amish Mennonites in the early 1900s. Several independent churches observe various levels of conservatism. In the most conservative congregations men wear long chin beards, short tapered hair, plain-crown, narrow-brimmed hats, sack coats with lapels and buttons, conventional pants, suspenders, and high-top shoes. Women wear head coverings with tie strings, bonnets, capes, aprons, and black stockings.

Beachy Amish Mennonites *(Church Amish, Automobile Amish, often called Amish Mennonites but not to be confused with earlier group.)*

This group withdrew from the Old Order Amish beginning in the 1920s with frequent accessions thereafter. Standards vary a great deal. Their general characteristics are:

Men: hair—short, combed straight back or parted in middle, cut off straight in back. Beard—short, either ear-to-ear or just on chin, mustaches in many churches. Hat—narrow brim, creased and pinched crown, worn mostly by older men. Pants—broadfalls in most conservative churches, otherwise conventional style. Suspenders—required in some churches, belts allowed in others. Vest—very rare. Work coat—store-bought with zipper.

Women: hair—uncut, center part, worn in bun. Head covering—square corners, always with tie strings, often with single, narrow pleat down back. Bonnets—very rare. Cape—rectangular style, usually worn daily. Apron—may or may not be required; a bib apron may replace cape and apron for daily wear. Coat—dark, short, with buttons. Stockings—black required in most but not all churches.

Solid color fabrics are the rule. Wristwatches are allowed in most churches, but plain, nonmetallic bands are usually specified.

Mennonites of Swiss Background

The Mennonite Church
(Old Mennonites, Conference Mennonites)

Mennonites originating from Switzerland had established communities in eastern Pennsylvania, Maryland, Virginia, and Ontario by 1800. They spread further west to Ohio and Indiana by 1850. This was the largest group of American Mennonites, the "Old" Mennonite Church.

Practices in plain clothing always varied considerably. Conferences in the East were more conservative (Lancaster, Franconia, Washington-Franklin, Virginia). There were also pockets of conservatism in Ontario, Oregon, Ohio, and elsewhere.

After a period of decline, plain clothing was reemphasized in the late 19th century. By the 1920s most conferences required the head covering and bonnet for women and strongly advocated the plain coat for men. In the East the cape dress, covering ties, and black stockings were further required of women. In the Midwest, where the plain coat was often worn only by the ministers, a campaign against neckties began in the 1880s. This movement was resisted at first in the East. In Lancaster Conference a bow tie was considered appropriate, even with a plain coat. By the 1940s Lancaster Conference strongly urged men to wear the plain coat without a tie.

Until the 1950s most Mennonite Church conferences prohibited cut hair, makeup, slacks, and shorts for women, and jewelry (including wedding bands) for both sexes. In the 1960s and '70s most Midwest conferences dropped these requirements, and conferences in the East began deemphasizing non-conformed dress until little was left by 1980. In the Lancaster Conference about 20 congregations still require the minimum standards of the 1950s (mentioned above) as well as women wearing their uncut hair up and the daily wearing of head coverings. Very few congregations in other conferences hold to this standard.

Conservative Mennonite Groups

In reaction to this drift many conservatively minded Mennonites withdrew from the larger conferences to form inde-

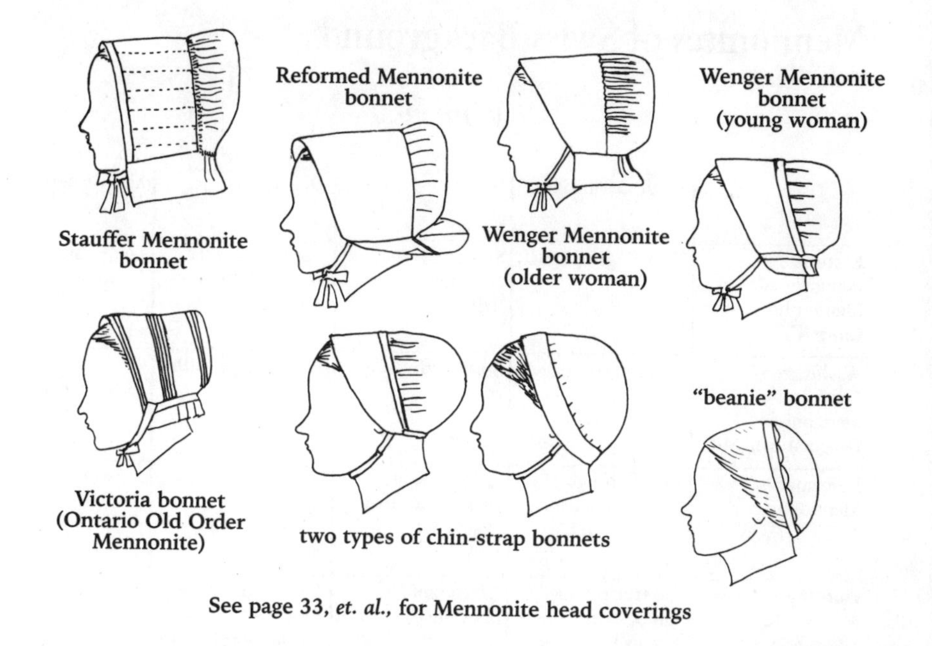

See page 33, *et. al.*, for Mennonite head coverings

pendent fellowships. The largest of these, the **Eastern Pennsylvania Mennonite Church,** withdrew from the Lancaster Conference in 1968. There are at least nine other similar groups and many unaffiliated congregations, some more conservative than the Eastern group and some less so. All are very similar in their general dress standards, except for the Washington-Franklin Conference which has held to older patterns of dress.

Several other earlier conservative withdrawals occurred in the Mennonite Church, the first being the **Reformed Mennonite Church** which began in 1785 in Lancaster County, Pennsylvania, but was not officially organized until 1812. They have preserved a very conservative style of dress, especially the women.

The **Stauffer** or **Pike Mennonites** originated in Lancaster County in 1845. The several different groups stemming from this division constitute the most conservative element in the Swiss Mennonite family.

In the late 19th century a number of regional groups withdrew from the Mennonite Church in reaction to mounting progressive tendencies. This began in Indiana in 1872, occurred in Ontario in

Mennonites of Swiss Background

Women

	Head Covering	Bonnet	Dress	Shawls and Coats
Eastern Pennsylvania Mennonite Church	Tie strings optional	Small with chin strap (often omitted)	Rectangular cape, skirt usually gored	Long, dark coats for winter
Washington-Franklin Mennonite (Hagerstown, MD)	Tie strings usually tied, often black	Small with tie strings	Pointed cape, with apron, gored skirt	Long, dark coats for winter
Reformed Mennonite	No tie strings, crown gathered onto front piece	Large, gray, with neck curtain that stands out from neck	Pointed cape, with apron; large peplum, usually gray	Shawl or long coat
Horning Mennonite (Weaverland Conference)[28]	Tie strings usually untied; white strings for younger, black for older[29]	(often omitted) Small, usually with chin strap	Usually rectangular cape, rarely pointed, apron rare, usually gored skirt	Various kinds of coats
Wenger Mennonite (Groffdale Conference)[30]	Tie strings tied for church; white strings for younger, black for older[31]	Fairly large with tie strings[32]	Pointed cape first worn at 16, apron at 18 (at church), pleated skirt	Shawl for church, coats usually for other times[33]
Virginia Old Order Mennonite[34]	White untied strings for younger; black tied strings for older[35]	Tie strings, bow at neckline	Pointed cape, not worn until baptism; aprons formerly rare, now more common	Shawls worn mostly by older women, coats and sweaters for younger
Ontario Old Order Mennonite[37] **(Woolwich Group)**	Strings mostly tied; white strings for younger, black strings for older[38]	Small, hard crown bonnet for winter, larger bonnet for summer[39]	Pointed cape and apron to church at 14, girls wear bib aprons daily	Shawl for church, coats usual for other times
Stauffer Mennonite[42]	Covers ears, always tied, strings may be black or white[43]	Very large, stitching on brim like slat bonnet, long neck curtain[44]	Pointed cape, apron; pinafore apron for girls until 16; pleated skirt	Coat not worn without shawl

Men

Hat	Hair	Suit coat	Necktie	Pants
Plain crown, narrow brim (often omitted)	Short, side part	Plain sack coat at conversion, frock coat for ordained	Not worn	Fly front, usually with belt
Plain crown, narrow brim	Short, side part	Plain frock coat at conversion	Not worn	Fly front with belt or suspenders
Plain crown, narrow brim	Short, side part	Plain frock coat at conversion	Small black bow tie	Fly front with belt or suspenders
Plain crown, narrow to wide brim, or pinched crown narrow brim, or omitted	Short, side part	Plain sack coat at marriage, frock coat for ministers and some non-ordained	Long ties were common for youth, now rare	Fly front with belt or suspenders, broadfalls for ordained
Pinched crown, narrow brim for younger, plain crown wider brim for older	Short, side part or combed front in bangs	Plain frock coat at marriage with plain vest	Bow ties were common for youth, now rare	Broadfalls with frock coat, fly front typical for work, suspenders
Plain or pinched crown, narrow to medium brim	Short, side part	Plain frock or sack coat at baptism or marriage, V-neck vest[36]	Long ties were common for youth, now rare	Fly front most common, some broadfalls, mostly suspenders, some belts among youth
Youth wear flat caps, married men plain crown, medium to wide brim[40]	Short, side part or combed front in bangs	Plain frock coat and plain vest at marriage or later[41]	Long ties worn by singles and some young marrieds	Suspenders, or bib overalls for work, broadfalls with frock coat
Plain crown, 4" brim	Cut off straight in back, usually center part, sometimes bangs	Plain frock coat and plain vest[45]	Not worn	Broadfalls with suspenders

1889, in Pennsylvania in 1893, and in Virginia in 1900. Dress was not a central issue in these divisions, but the resulting **Old Order Mennonite** groups that formed stressed the importance of distinctive attire.

In all the larger Old Order Mennonite communities there have been divisions over automobile use. The largest such group is the Horning Mennonite Church of Pennsylvania. The car-driving Old Orders are now very similar in dress to the conservative groups which emerged from the Mennonite Church after 1950. There were also small groups who withdrew from the larger Old Order Mennonite bodies to form more traditional churches.

Nearly all conservative Mennonites of Swiss origin share at least two characteristics: printed fabrics are allowed, and men are clean-shaven. The chart on the next page demonstrates some of the differences in several representative groups.

Mennonites of Dutch Background

Mennonites from Holland extended into Russia during the lifetime of Menno Simons. From there many moved to Russia. Beginning in 1874, Russian Mennonites emigrated en masse to North America.

Old Colony Mennonites in Latin America

The most conservative Russian Mennonites settled in Manitoba, and the most conservative of these, the Old Colony Mennonites, largely moved to Mexico in the 1920s. From Mexico some Old Colony people established settlements in Belize, Bolivia, and Paraguay.

The traditional Old Colony dress practices are:

Men's everyday dress—bib overalls, long-sleeved shirt, cowboy hat. Men's Sunday dress—conventional, dark sack coat (often with bib overalls), dark-colored shirt, no tie. Ministers—long, black, conventional frock coat (double- or single-breasted), black shirt, knee-length black boots, full-crowned, black bill cap.

Women—center parted hair in braided coils. Large, fringed head shawl (black for married, white for single) often with floral border; some wear a lightweight scarf tied behind the ears. Older women

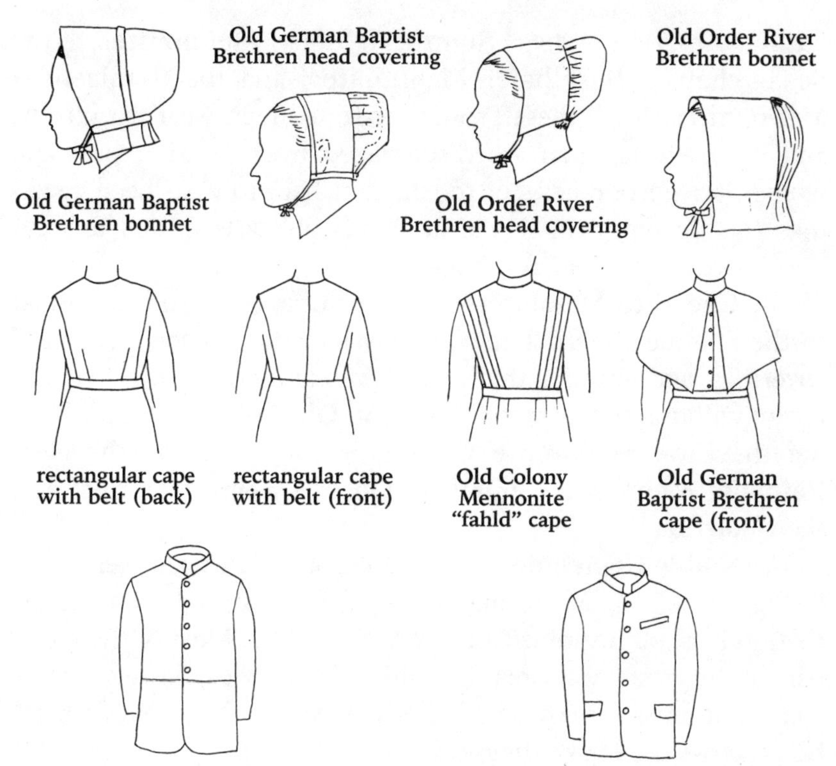

wear mähtz, a black lace cap with a tightly ruffled ridge extending from ear to ear across the top of the head; it is usually worn beneath the head shawl and usually just for church. Wide-brimmed hats adopted in Mexico for outdoor wear. Heavy hair nets extended over forehead very common. Dresses have rectangular-styled capes called "fahlds," with multiple vertical pleats worn by married women (not strictly observed in many cases). Horizontal tuck pleats on skirts and aprons. All black clothing for Sunday; dark prints typical for other times. Black stockings the rule; white now often seen, as well as sandals and no stockings.

Canadian Russian Mennonite Groups

The Old Colony Mennonites who remained in Canada or returned there from Mexico are not as traditional in their dress. This is also true of several other related groups both in Canada and

Latin America; the **Sommerfelder Mennonites,** the **Saskatchewan Bergthaler Mennonites,** and the **Reinlaender Mennonites.** In all these groups, ordained men wear frock coats and black shirts, men are discouraged from wearing ties, and women are encouraged not to cut their hair, to wear head coverings (taking the form of various kinds of scarves), and to wear dresses rather than slacks or shorts.

The **Chortitza Mennonites of Manitoba** had been very similar to the Sommerfelders, but now only half the women wear head coverings, and neckties are present even among the ministry. The recent withdrawals from the **Canadian Old Colony Church** forming the **Zion Mennonite Church** in Manitoba and the **New Reinland Mennonite Church** in Ontario seem to be much like the Chortitza.

The **Kleine Gemeinde** are another group of Russian Mennonite background. In Manitoba the group adopted the name, **Evangelical Mennonite Conference,** in 1952. Most of the members of the group now dress in fashionable clothes; however, some congregations stress the head covering (taking the form of a black band across the top of the head in one church).

Just prior to the change in name, some conservative Kleine Gemeinde moved to Mexico. Some of them then moved to Belize, Costa Rica, Paraguay, Oklahoma, Nova Scotia, and back to Manitoba. The men wear conservative, dark suits without neckties for church. Women do not cut their hair and wear it up. Their head coverings are three-cornered, black scarves, and they wear simple, modest dresses. The **Emmanuel Mennonite Church** of Meade, Kansas, of Kleine Gemeinde background, is similar to the Evangelical Mennonite Conference.

Other Russian Mennonite Groups

The Church of God in Christ Mennonite (Holdemans) was started by a Mennonite of Swiss background in Ohio, although the great majority of Holdemans are of Manitoba and Kansas Russian Mennonite background. Men have short beards and short hair. Conventional lapel coats are worn without ties. Women do not cut their hair and wear it up. Black, three-cornered scarves are worn for

Hutterites

	Men			Women				
Group	Beard	Boy's Cap	Coat	Head Scarf	Cap	Dress Fabric	Bodice	Apron
Lehrerleut (AB, SK, MT)	Usually no mustache	Stiff with circular crown	Buttons, no collar	Large dots	Printed fabric	Bright plaids popular	Sleeveless	Tied in front
Dariusleut (AB, SK, MT)	Mustache optional	Black, conventional cap	Hooks, no collar, or else turnover collar	Small or medium dots, sometimes no dots	Printed material	Darker colors	Traditionally with sleeves (long or 3/4 length)	Tied in front or back
Schmeideleut (MB, SD)	With mustache	Various kinds of bill caps	Snaps, turnover collar	Medium dots	Solid colors (usually white for women, black for girls)	Bright prints	Sleeveless	Tied in back, sometimes absent
Arnoldleut (NY, CT, PA, England)	Usually with mustache	Not usually worn	Snaps, turnover collar	Medium dots	Only for elementary school girls	Solid blue for many occasions, also prints	Sleeveless	Not a part of usual dress

church. Most women wear a scarf folded into the shape of a cap for everyday. Simple dresses are worn, but they are not of a uniform cut. Slack, shorts, makeup, and jewelry are forbidden for women.

The Fairview Oklahoma Church of God (Apostolische Brudergemeinde, the Breadbreakers, or the Penner Group) was started by Russian Mennonites about 1865.

Men wear long, untrimmed beards, no neckties, and dark, conventional suits. Women do not cut their hair, wear scarves as head coverings, and wear simple, modest dresses.

Hutterites

The Hutterites branched from Swiss Anabaptism in 1528, then lived in various places in eastern Europe until they settled in South Dakota in 1874. Many moved to Canada around the time of World War I. The Hutterian Society of Brothers began independently in Germany in 1920 and united with the North American Hutterites in 1930. After living in England and Paraguay they now have three communities in the eastern U.S.

There are four distinct Hutterite groups. Some dress characteristics apply to all groups:

Men—fairly short hair. Beards grown at either baptism or marriage. Cowboy hats for work, plain black hats for church and formal occasions. Caps for boys. Black coats and pants. Long-sleeved shirts of printed fabrics. Elastic suspenders. Special frock coats for ministers and others for some occasions.

Women—hair parted in the middle and made into rolls looping around ears and fastening to bun. Three-cornered, black and white polka-dot scarves (sometimes with embroidered edges) are worn over close-fitting caps with chin straps. The caps are sometimes worn alone, especially by small girls. Dresses consist of light-colored, elbow-length blouses, separate bodices (which may be sleeveless or long- or short-sleeved), skirts (with horizontal tucks near the hem), and aprons. The last three items may be matching or of contrasting material. One-piece dresses are worn until age 10, and special dresses are worn for various occasions.

Brethren (German Baptists, Dunkers, Dunkards)

Begun in Germany in 1708 and transplanted to America within a few years, the largest body adopted the name "Church of the Brethren" in 1908. The Old German Baptist Brethren separated from the main body in 1881 to preserve the old ways, as did the Dunkard Brethren in 1926.[46] There have also been a number of smaller divisions within these three groups.[47] Plain dress rapidly vanished in the Church of the Brethren after 1920. Several congregations in Pennsylvania still maintain some conservative dress standards. Many older women continue to wear head coverings.

Brethren groups have traditionally promoted beards, but in even the most conservative groups only the ordained men are actually required to wear them. Children are not expected to dress in the full order of the church until baptism. Printed fabrics have always been allowed.

River Brethren and Brethren in Christ

The River Brethren movement began in Lancaster County, Pennsylvania, about 1780. In the 1850s there was a three-way division producing the Old Order River Brethren, the Brethren in Christ, and the United Zion Church.

The Brethren in Christ emphasized plain dress until the 1950s. In the 1940s most men wore lapel coats without neckties, a few wore plain coats, and some wore standing collar vests with lapel coats. In some areas women wore cape dresses and head

Brethren

Men

	Hat and Hair	Beard	Sunday Coat	Pants
Conservative element in Church of the Brethren (PA)	No requirements, usually short, tapered	A few worn out of conviction	Usually lapel coat, no tie, some plain sack coats	Fly front with belt
Dunkard Brethren	Narrow brim; plain crown in some areas; tapered hair; center part encouraged	Commonly worn, often with mustache	Plain sack coat	Fly front with belt
Old German Baptist Brethren[48]	Plain crown, medium brim, blocked hair, center or no part	Required of ministry, no mustache	Plain frock, vest	Broadfall with belt or susupenders
Old Brethren German Baptist and Old Order German Baptist	Plain crown, wide brim, blocked hair, center or no part	Required of ministry	Plain frock, vest	Broadfall with suspenders
Old Order River Brethren	Plain crown, wide brim, block hair, center part	Worn by all members, often with mustache	Plain frock, vest frequent	Usually broadfall with suspenders, some fly front with belt

Women

	Hair and Covering	Bonnet	Cape and Apron	Coat and Shawl	Stockings
Conservative element in Church of the Brethren (PA)	Side part, covering with no strings	Rare	Capes rare, no aprons	Conventional coats	Conventional
Dunkard Brethren	Covering with strings, often tied	Common in some churches, small, chin strap	Capes required in some churches, no aprons	Conventional coats	Usually conventional
Old German Baptist Brethren	Center part or no part, covering over ears, always tied	Large with curtain and ties	3-corner cape, apron required	Mostly tailored shawls	Usually conventional, black in some areas
Old Brethren German Baptist and Old Order German Baptist	Center part, covering over ears, always tied	Large slat type with ties and curtain	3-corner cape, apron required	Folded shawls	Black
Old Order River Brethren	Center part, opaque covering tied	Large with curtain	3-corner cape, apron always worn	Coats and folded shawls	Black

coverings with tie strings, but a covering worn with otherwise conventional dress was more typical by 1950. Few churches stressed plain dress by the 1970s. Two small conservative groups withdrew from the Brethren in Christ: the Calvary Holiness Church in 1963 and the Evangelical Brethren in 1970.[49]

The United Zion Church is similar to the Brethren in Christ but still requires the head covering for worship services.

The Old Order River Brethren still maintain traditional plain dress.

Other Related and Similar Churches

United Christian Church

The United Christian Church withdrew from the United Brethren Church in Pennsylvania in 1865. They have not had a specified garb, but simplicity is emphasized. Some men do not wear neckties, and many women wear their uncut hair up with a head covering and/or bonnet.

Amana Church Society *(Community of True Inspiration)*

Begun in Germany in 1714 and reestablished in America in 1842, this group is now located in a cluster of villages in Iowa. Women currently wear traditional garb only for worship. This consists of a black cap tied beneath the chin (worn with modern hair styles), a dark-colored shawl-kerchief, and an apron worn with a simple dark dress. A large, light-colored sunbonnet with a long neck curtain had been an Amana trademark. All plain dress for men disappeared by 1900.

Apostolic Christians

Begun in Switzerland in 1832 among the Reformed Church and Mennonites, the first Apostolic Christians came to America in 1847. The largest group emphasizes conservative dress. Men wear conventional dark suits and ties. Extremes are avoided. Women wear uncut hair pinned up and do not wear makeup, jewelry, slacks, or shorts. Head coverings (usually black lace veils) are worn for worship. Many women wear a black strip of cloth across the top of the head for everyday.

The German Apostolic Christian Church divided from the main body in the 1930s. They are generally very conservative in their dress. The women wear simple, hat-like head coverings and black stockings.

The Christian Apostolic Church divided from the German group in the 1950s and '60s. In conservatism they are midway between the other two groups. A progressive group divided from the main body of Apostolic Christians in 1907. They are referred to as Nazarenes and do not stress simple dress.

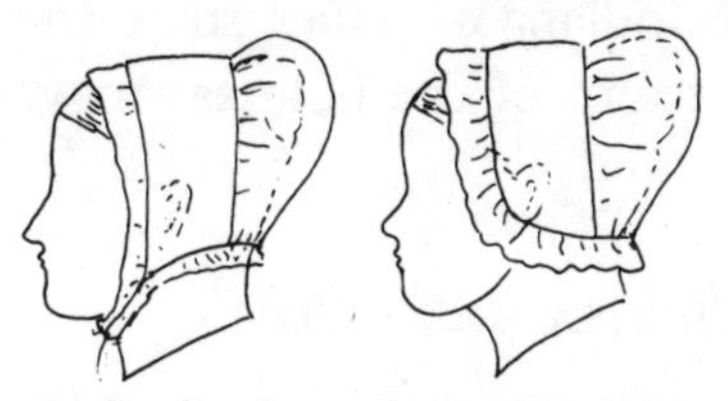

Quaker head coverings 1800-1900

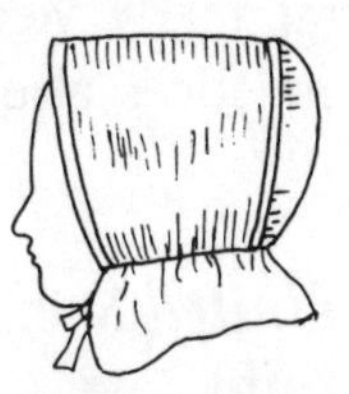

Shaker bonnet

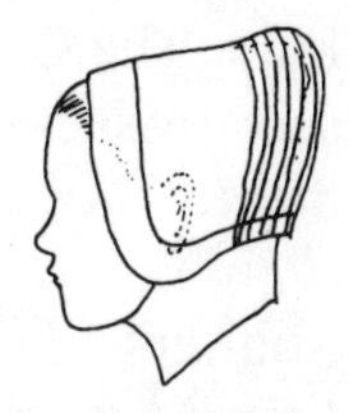

Shaker head covering

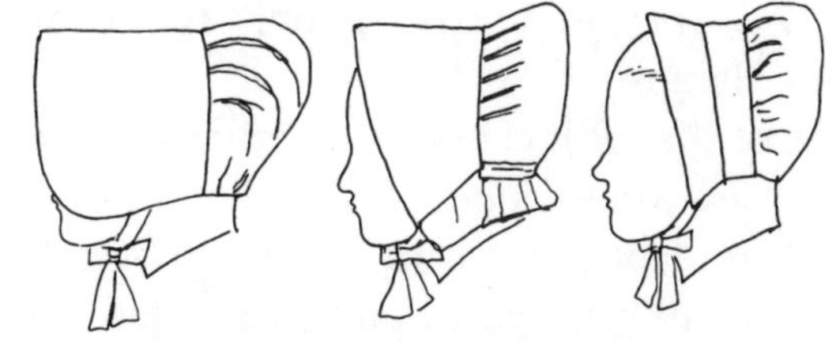

Quaker bonnets 1800-1920

Shaker dress with kerchief

Shaker dress with cape

Quaker kerchief and shawl

The Society of Friends *(Quakers)*

This movement began in England in the 1640s and spread to America in 1656. All through the 19th century a characteristic pattern of plain dress was recognized as distinctly Quaker. This consisted of a wide-brimmed hat, a standing collar coat and vest for men, and a large, plain bonnet, a white cap, a white kerchief, a light shawl, and a plain dress for women. Gray and brown were the predominate colors. This distinctive costume vanished rapidly in most areas after 1900.

In the Philadelphia Orthodox Yearly Meeting (Arch Street) and among the Conservative (Wilburite) Yearly Meetings some were still wearing plain garb in the 1950s. A few dozen plain Quakers still survive, scattered mostly in Ohio, Pennsylvania, Virginia, and

Iowa. The Central Yearly Meeting in Indiana observes some conservative dress practices after the pattern of the holiness movement.

Shakers *(The United Society of Believers in Christ's Second Appearing)*

The Shakers began in England in the 1740s and came to America in 1774. They now exist in only two communities in Maine and New Hampshire.

During most of the 19th century the following dress practices were observed. Men wore wide-brimmed, flat-crowned hats, long frock coats with no lapels but with small turnover collars, long-waisted, button-to-the-neck vests, and narrow fall trousers. Neck cloths or stocks were sometimes worn. The hair was worn in short bangs in front and long in back. Men were clean-shaven. After 1880 beards and lapel coats without ties became common. After about 1900 most men wore fashionable dress.

Women wore white caps with ties, palm leaf or straw bonnets, white collars, three-cornered kerchiefs, aprons, dresses with pleated skirts, and long cloaks for winter. In the late 19th century tailored rounded capes began replacing the kerchief, ties were omitted from caps, women wore padded black combs in their hair to keep their caps away from their faces, and the separate white collars and aprons were omitted. The New York communities dropped all distinctive dress in the early 1900s. Currently capes are worn by all Shaker sisters, but caps are worn more in New Hampshire than in Maine. Bonnets are rarely worn.

Notes

Chapter 2—The Religious Basis for Plain Clothing

1. Matthew 7:14
2. II Thessalonians 2:3
3. Romans 12:2
4. I Peter 1:4
5. John 15:19
6. I John 2:15-17
7. I Corinthians 6:17
8. I Peter 2:9, 11
9. I Peter 5:5
10. Luke 8:35
11. I Timothy 2:2, 10
12. I Peter 3:3, 4

Chapter 3—Where Did the Plain Patterns Come from?

1. Melvin Gingerich, *Mennonite Attire through Four Centuries* (Breinigsville, PA, 1970), passim; John A. Hostetler, "Amish Costume: Its European Origins," American-German Review, 22 (August/September, 1956), 11-14; Don Yoder, "Sectarian Costume Research in the United States, *Forms upon the Frontier* (Logan, Utah, 1969), 41-75.
2. Eugene Kraybill, *Seven Hundred Churches* (Lancaster, PA, 1985), 17.
3. *Johannes Kessler Sabbata,* (St. Gallen, 1902), 147. In 1525 John Kessler spoke of the very earliest Anabaptists, "They shun costly clothing and despise expensive food and drink, clothe themselves with coarse cloth and cover their heads with broad felt hats."

Sebastian Frank, *Chronica* (Strasbourg, 1531). A statement is made that Moravian Anabaptists had definite specifications on dress, and that some Anabaptists had a ruling on how many pleats the apron must have.

Thieleman J. van Braght, *Martyrs Mirror* (Scottdale, PA, 1944), 466. Reference is made to a man coming from Moravia to a believer in Austria "clothed as a brother" (1544).

Heinrich Bullinger, *Des Widertäufferen Ursprung* (Zurich, 1561), leaf 20 recto. A group of Anabaptists was described who ". . . make rules about clothing, whereof, of what form and shape, and how long, wide, or big they shall be. Here they reject all costly clothing and ornamentation." Some scholars feel that this reference does not apply to the main group of Anabaptists.

Harold S. Bender, "The Strasburg Discipline of 1568," *Mennonite Quarterly Review* (January 1927), 57-66. At an international gathering of Anabaptists, a list of directives was drawn up: "Article 20. Tailors and seamstresses shall hold to the plain and simple style and shall stay by the present form of our regulation concerning apparel and make nothing for pride's sake. Other translations say, "Tailors and seamstresses shall abide by the plain and simple custom of the land."

William McGrath, *Christlicher Ordnung* or *Christian Discipline* (Aylmer, Ontario, 1966), 15. Some versions of the Strasbourg Discipline further add, "shaving off the beard or trimming the hair of the head in stylish ways shall not be permitted."

"Concept of Cologne," *The Mennonite Encyclopedia, I* (Scottdale, PA , 1955), 663- 64. At a 1591 meeting of Swiss and Dutch Anabaptist it was not deemed possible to make a statement on dress that would apply to all locations, but a statement was made which required simplicity of attire and warned against elaborate attire which "resembles the world more than it show Christian humility." It also admonished believers to be a light to the world in their simple clothing and all their deeds.

Dr. Gustav Bossert, *Sources on the History of the Anabaptists,* I (Leipzig, 1930), 691, 741, 806. Several references to distinctive Anabaptist dress are given: in 1598 Conrad Wertz was described as wearing Anabaptist clothing, and Matthew Kappel was regarded as an Anabaptist on account of his clothing. A 1608 incident tells of a man coming from Moravia who was not considered an Anabaptist because of his clothing and speech. In

1617 it is said Christopher Reichlin came home wearing Anabaptist clothing.

Hans Latscher poem, written by a Swiss Anabaptist in 1662, translated by John Ruth in an unpublished manuscript, *The Earth is the Lord's.* "Of clothes there is no lacking with much unneedful pride, And manifold silk ribbons and trim of every kind, As our own age has now disclosed, to which the Lord God is opposed. Those who such things are leaving much money can be saving. There would be goodly colors that by themselves do grow: Such are the ones for wearing. We find it written so. Sheep wool itself has varied hue which is quite inexpensive too: One could, to this submitting, Still dress in manner fitting."

Georg Thromann, a Reformed clergyman, writing of the Anabaptists, *Probier-Stein* (Bern, 1693), 389. Translation by John Ruth is an unpublished manuscript, *The Earth is the Lord's.* "In their distinguishing themselves in outward clothing from all other honest people, do they not thereby make it understood that they are not averse to being recognized among the people, so that one can immediately say 'This is an Anabaptist?' Never imagine that the true fear of God consists in this or that manner of dressing (such as wearing nothing around the neck, no pleated trousers, etc.)."

C. Henry Smith, *The Mennonite Immigration to Pennsylvania in the 18th Century* (Norristown, PA, 1929), 60-68. In 1709 Laurens Hendricks, A Dutch Mennonite pastor, described Swiss Anabaptist refugees wearing "long and unshaven beards, disordered clothing, great shoes which were heavily hammered with iron and large nails."

4. Menno Simons, *The Complete Writings of Menno Simons c. 1496-1561* (Scottdale, PA, 1956), 377. In the writing, "True Christian Faith" of 1541, Menno condemned hypocrites. "They say that they believe, and yet also, there are no limits nor bonds to their accursed haughtiness, foolish pride and pomp; they parade in silks, velvet, costly clothes, gold rings, chains, silver belts, pins and buttons, curiously adorned shirts, shawls collars, aprons, velvet shoes, slippers, and such like foolish finery." (The English translation of clothing items may not refer to those we know by the same name today.)

5. Thieleman J. Van Braght, *Martyrs Mirror* (Scottdale, PA, 1944), 495, 898. In 1550 a Dutch Anabaptist martyr being burned at the stake said that if he could name twenty fellow believers in the crowd he would not do so. Another incident in Holland in 1572 involves a man who pressed his way through a crowd before the authorities could seize him.

6. C. N. Wybrands, *Het Menniste Zusje* (Amsterdam, 1913), 35. The 1659 dress regulations of the Old Flemish Mennonites forbade crimson linen, high-heeled shoes, clothes of the latest style or worldly fashion, starched underwear stiffened with bones, earrings, long hair for men, or cutting or shaving the head according to the worldly style.

M. Simon Friederich Rues, *Aufrichtige Nachrichten von dem Gegenwortigen Zustande der Mennoniten oder Taufgesinnten . . . in den vereinigten Neiederlanden* (1743). Referring to one group of conservative Dutch Mennonites, "It is to be sure true the Groninger are somewhat strict in clothing and all of them wear black clothing and also insist on the long beards although their preachers complain that this tradition ornament is being more and more laid aside by the younger brethren and the faces are shaved smooth."

7. John Martin Vincent, *Costume and Conduct in the Laws of Basel, Bern and Zurich 1370-1800* (Baltimore, 1935).

8. See note 3.

9. The dress of rural England was especially simple; no elaborate folk costumes developed there. This simplicity was transferred to America and thus was probably supportive to the convictions of Pennsylvania's plain people.

10. Alma Oakes and Margot Hamilton Hill, *Rural Costume* (London, 1970). Note the similarity in men's costumes in Fig. 41 p. 30 (18th century France), Fig. 44 p. 32 (18th century Norway) Fig. 46 p. 33 (Italy, 1769), Fig. 62 p. 37 (Sweden, 1823) and the women's costumes in Fig. 125 p. 62 (Netherlands, 1657), Fig. 133 p. 66 (Spain, 1799), Fig. 139 p. 68 (North Netherlands, 1811), Fig. 147 p. 71 (Sweden, 1827), Fig. 295 p. 176 (England, late 18th century), Fig. 301 p. 178 (England, 1820).

11. James Snowden, *The Folk Dress of Europe* (New York, 1979), 9-10.

12. Anne Buck, *Dress in Eighteenth Century England* (New York, 1979), 127.

13. Anne Buck, *Dress in Eighteenth Century England* (New York, 1979), 49, 122.

C. Willet and Phillis Cunnington, *Handbook of English Costume in the Eighteenth Century*

Amish—LaGrange County, Indiana.

(London, 1957), 353. "The milk-maid's chip hat, rescued for a time from old women and servant girls to adorn heads of the first fashion"; as recorded in *The Connoisseur,* 1754.

14. Phillis Cunnington, *Costume of Household Servants* (New York, 1974), 172; Phillis Cunnington and Catherine Lucas, *Occupational Costume in England* (London, 1967), 28.

Claudia Kidwell, *Suiting Everyone* (Washington, 1974), 21. Speaking of the 18th century she writes, "Standing apart from the prevalent male dress would be those in trousers: seamen, farmers in from the country, some apprentice boys, and others of the 'meaner sort.'" Mention is made of fifty gentlemen actors who disguised themselves in trousers and jackets when they took part in the Stamp Act violence of 1765.

15. C. Willet and Phillis Cunnington, *Handbook of English Costume in the Nineteenth Century* (Boston, 1970), 51. In 1830, *The Gentlemen's Magazine of Fashion* referred to the fly front as "an indelicate and disgusting fashion."

16. Thomas P. McCarthy, *Guide to the Catholic Sisterhoods in the United States* (Washington, 1964). See especially Sisters of Charity orders established by Elizabeth Ann Seton, pages 212, 214, & 218.

Phillis Cunnington and Catherine Lucas, *Charity Costumes* (New York, 1978), 20: "The attire of objects of charity was originally above everything else plain as a mark of humility." Page 30: "To be old fashioned in dress is associated with being humble . . ." Many of the costumes illustrated closely resemble plain dress.

17. Alma Oakes and Margot Hamilton Hill, *Rural Costume* (New York 1970), 172, 174. Figures 287, 289, & 290, from the 17th century *Roxburghe Ballads,* show rural women wearing the kerchief, jacket bodice, and apron. Fig. 292 p. 174 (1640, England) is similar as in Fig. 125 p. 62 (1657, Netherlands).

18. Claudia Kidwell, "Short Gowns," *Dress,* 4 (1978), 30-65. Shows persistence of 17th century style of separate bodice and skirt among 18th and early 19th century commoners.

Claudia Kidwell. *Suiting Everyone* (Washington, 1974), 33. "The short gown, worn with a petticoat, was a serviceable garb having no fashionable pretensions; hence it was worn with little change over the years. . . It must have been a common form of female dress, particular in the rural areas."

Phyllis Cunnington, *Costume of Household Servants* (New York, 1974), passim. A number of illustrations show working women in caps, kerchiefs,and aprons during the first three decades of the 19th century. One illustration (137) also shows a jacket bodice in 1829.

19. *Minutes of the Annual Meetings of the Old German Baptist Brethren* (Winona Lake, IN, 1981), 35.

20. Catharine Fennelly, *The Garb of Country New Englanders* (Sturbridge, MA, 1966), 5.

21. C. Willet and Phillis Cunnington, *Handbook of English Costume in the Nineteenth Century* (Boston, 1970), passim. In this and other costume books there are no references or illustrations of standing collar coats in common use after 1800; Aileen Riberiro, *A Visual History of Costume, the Eighteen Century* (London and New York, 1983). All but a few pictures showing men's coats during the last quarter of the 18th century show turnover collars.

Melvin Gingerich, *Mennonite Attire through Four Centuries* (Breinigsville, PA, 1970), 41-47. The author illustrates and describes two Mennonite coats from Ontario. One from ca. 1790, the other from 1856. They are said to be typical of coats worn by non-Mennonites of the time. The standing collar found on both coats would have been old-fashioned in the 1790s and archaic in the 1850s. The combination of the standing collar and the absence of outside pockets in the earlier coat was distinctive. This writer arrived at different conclusions than Gingerich from studying portraits and costume histories (many published since 1970). This writer also found it impossible to determine what kind of coat collars are illustrated in most of Lewis Miller's drawings, which Gingerich makes several references to. The four coats in the York County, Pennsylvania Historical Society that Gingerich mentions would seem too limited an example to arrive at a broad conclusion.

22. Frederick Lewis Allen, *Only Yesterday* (New York, 1931). 73-101.

23. Redmond Coyngham, *The History of the Mennonites and Aymenists* (1830). Palatine immigrants, thought to be Amish or Mennonites, are described from an undocumented source said to be from 1707. Long beards and long red caps are ascribed to the men and short petticoats and uncovered heads (except for a string passing around the head) for the women. "The dress of both male and female was domestic, quite plain, made of coarse material after an old fashion of their own."

John Ruth, *The Earth is the Lord's* (unpublished manuscript). In 1717 Isaac Taylor, a surveyor, referred to Lancaster Mennonites as "long-bearded Switzers."

I.D. Rupp, *History of Lancaster County* (Lancaster, PA, 1844), 194. In 1727 Pennsylvania Governor Gordon received a delegation representing, "a large number of Germans peculiar in their dress, religion, and notions of political government."

J. Max Hark, trans., *Chronicon Ephratense* (Lancaster, PA, 1899), 41, 55. In 1727 Israel Eckerlin was advised to move from Germantown to the Conestoga (Lancaster County) because the people there lived in great simplicity. He adhered to the Mennonites for a time "because their simplicity of dress pleased us." Conrad Beissel, the founder of the Ephrata Cloister, at first followed the humble example of the Mennonites in his dress and manner of living but later was persuaded to dress like a Quaker after which the rest of the solitary brethren followed his example.

William J. Hinke, *History of the Goschenhoppen Reformed Charge* (Lancaster, PA, 1920), 38. In 1730 Jedidiah Andrews remarked that Mennonites in the Pequea settlement (Lancaster County) did not shave their heads. It was fashionable at this time for men to shave their heads and wear fancy powdered wigs. The reference may also refer to shaving the beard.

"Minutes of the Provincial Council of Pennsylvania," VI, 659-60, *Pennsylvania Archives, First Series*, II, 514-15. In 1755 Conrad Weiser made the statement, "I had two or three long beards in my company, one a Menonist."

William Stevens Perry, ed., *Historical Collections Relating to the American Colonial Church*, II, 315. Thomas Burton, a Church of England missionary in Lancaster, Pennsylvania, said of the Mennonites in 1760, "With their doctrine and principles I am not acquainted but find them in many things to agree with those of the Quakers. They use the same mode of dress, refuse to put off the hat, or show respect to superiors."

J.B.S., *The Alert Traveler through Europe and America* (Altona, Germany, 1777). In 1761

Old German Baptist Brethren

this pietist writer described several Pennsylvania plain groups. Concerning the Quakers: "Their clothing is modest, neat, and of the best material"; the Brethren: "Their clothing is middle-class. Most of the men wear beards"; the Mennonites: "They wear plain clothing; proud colors may not be worn by them. Most of the men wear beards."

Morgan Edwards, *Materials Towards a History of the Baptists of Pennsylvania* (Philadelphia, 1770), 74-79, 95. Describing the Brethren (Dunkers): "They use great plainness of language and dress, like the Quakers. They commonly wear their beards"; concerning the Mennonites: "Some of them yet wear their beards . . . They, like the Dunkers, use great plainness of speech and dress. This last is so capital with them that some have been expelled from their societies for having buckles to their shoes and pocket holes to their coats."

Thomas A. Hughes, *A Journal* (1778-1789)(Cambridge, England, 1947), 88-89. Writing in 1780 about Lancaster Mennonites, "They never wear buckles or metal buttons."

Lancaster Journal, August 19, 1801. An ad appeared offering a reward for Jacob Shinour who ran away from Elias Albright wearing, "a claret coloured cloth coat, made in the Mennonite fashion."

Elizabeth Clarke Kieffer, "The First Native American Dancer," *Pennsylvania Dutchman* (June, 1954), 36. John Durang, during a tour, described some Lancaster Countians in about 1800, "This part of the country or neighborhood is generally inhabited by a sect of people called Manistes or Dunkerds. They are Germans. The aged men wear their beards very long and clothes very plain and generally homespun of their own manufacture."

Anonymous, "Gestaltdes reichs Gottes unter den Deutschen in Amerika," *Evangelisches Magazine, III* (April-June, 1814), 135. A Lutheran writer wrote of the Mennonites, "The old preachers who preached only . . . customs and styles of clothing . . . "

Gertrude Mohlin Ziegler, *The Ziegler Family and Related Families in Pennsylvania* (Zelienople, PA, 1978), 36. In 1819 Abraham Ziegler, a Mennonite from the Franconia area of Pennsylvania, engaged a German tailor for his new settlement at Harmony, Pennsylvania, and ordered a coat in the Mennonite style.

Mennonite Quarterly Review (January, 1932), 52-53. In an 1837 letter Jacob Risser told of a conversation with a Mennonite minister from Ohio who stated, " 'I would not believe that one could be a true Christian and wear such a hat and coat.' (He referred to some young people sitting near us who were still wearing the ordinary hat and coat as commonly worn, since they were not yet baptized although they were already in young manhood.)"

Elizabeth Bender, trans., "A Letter of John H. Oberholtzer to Unamed Friends in Germany, 1849," *Mennonite Quarterly Review* (October, 1972), 401. John Oberholtzer accused the Mennonite Church, "But allow me to tell you what the most of our preachers in part look at to recognize a true Mennonite—it is the 'coat.' If it has the right cut, then in the opinion of many, all is right."

Herald of Truth (October, 1868), 149-150. Speaking of the Mennonite Church, "Only our denomination and a few others are left to uphold simple dress in practice."

Cornelius Janzen, *Sammlung von Notizen Uber Amerika* (Danzig, 1872), 24. In 1871 Peter Wiebe noted that among a group of Mennonites in Missouri, "Also they hold fast to old-fashioned costume and clothes, especially sisters of the church who nearly all dressed alike . . ."

Herald of Truth (July, 1880), 128. A Mennonite writer noted the Brethren (Dunker) idea of having a plain clothing store and thought it would be a good thing for the Mennonites as well.

When photographs were first introduced in the mid-19th century, the plain people denounced them as graven images (some still do). Nonetheless there are many extant photos from the 1800s showing Mennonites in plain dress. One may assume that the most conservative members did not have their pictures taken; therefore there is no photographic record of their appearance.

There is an abundance of 19th century wedding photos of fashionably dressed couples who came from plain homes but had not accepted the plain way themselves. The restrictions of the church did not govern those who had not yet been baptized. It is quite

Hutterites, Saskatchewan

common to find Mennonite portraits of the 1880-1910 period showing a plainly dressed woman with a conventionally dressed man (the opposite is often true of Brethren portraits). There are also many family portraits, some quite recent, which show plainly dressed parents with large families of fashionably dressed children.

24. Jacob Stauffer, *Geschicht-Büchlein* (Scottdale, PA, 1922), 268. In the first discipline of the Stauffer Mennonite Church in 1849 "double coats" and "cut-out coats" (the meaning of these German expressions is unclear) were among the worldly fashions that were not allowed. Fashionable hair styles were especially condemned.

25. Robert H. Billigmeier and Fred Altschuler Picard, ed. and trans., *The Old Land and the New. The Journals of Two Swiss Families in America in the 1820s* (Minneapolis, 1965), 157-61. In 1821 a young girl wrote her parents about the surprisingly elaborate dress and homes of some Lancaster County Mennonites.

John Ruth, *Maintaining the Right Fellowship* (Scottdale, PA, 1984), 227. John Oberholtzer stated that in the 1830s, Franconia Mennonite candidates for baptism were no longer required to wear plain coats.

Mennonite Quarterly Review (January, 1932), 51-54. In 1841 Jacob Krehbiel wrote to Mennonites in Europe, " . . . in some American Mennonite congregations too much emphasis is placed upon outward forms . . . In many places in Pennsylvania there is no difference between the costume worn by the Mennonites and that worn by other people. But this is not the case in all the congregations, either in Pennsylvania or in other states, as well as in Canada, since in some places more attention is devoted to this point than at others."

D. S. Gorter, ed., *Godsdienstige Lektuur voor Doopsgezinden, 5* (Sneek, The Netherlands, 1854), 294. Two Dutch Mennonites visiting northern Indiana in 1853 reported, "The strictness in clothing and other outward things is not as strict among the Mennonites as among the Amish brethren and the Tunkers, who generally distinguish themselves by the beard and in other ways. Only our brothers from Switzerland are a little stricter in this. Although they are generally humble in appearance, they live completely free. They do not mark themselves by a particular garb, attachment to color or other things; even the baptismal candidates are not dressed alike and communion and feetwashing are attended by each in his customary clothing."

John M. Brenneman, *Herald of Truth* (September, 1864), 56. A writer from Ohio reported that some members from Indiana had departed from the Old Mennonite way of dress.

Daniel Brenneman, *Herald of Truth* (September, 1872), 139. The writer regrets the loss of plain dress among Mennonites in the East.

26. John B. Mast, ed. and trans., *The Letters of the Amish Division* (Oregon City, Oregon, 1950), 42, 66. Jacob Amman, founder of the Amish, writes in 1693, "If anyone desires to conform to this world, by trimming the beard, by wearing long hair and attractive apparel, and will not confess that it is unrighteous, he shall be justly punished; for God is not pleased with the proud." It was fashionable for men to have their hair (real or artificial) flowing over their shoulders at this time. Gerhard Roosen, a north German (Dutch) Mennonite, wrote a letter in 1697 to the Anabaptist churches in Alsace warning them not to accept Jacob Amman's strict rules on dress. He mentions enforced patterns of hats, clothes, stockings, shoes, and the hair of the head.

John C. Wenger, *History of the Mennonites of the Franconia Conference* (Telford, PA, 1937), 399. Three bishops of the Franconia Mennonite Conference wrote to Mennonites in Holland in 1773. They explained that they held to no human regulations but, " . . . As to the Amish . . . they hold very fast to the outward and ancient institutions."

McGrath, *Christlicher Ordnung*, 28. The 1779 Amish discipline of Essingen, Germany, forbids that young men shave or cut their hair in a worldly style, and that no worldly clothing be worn including flowered, checked, or any loud-colored clothing.

27. Donald Durnbaugh, "Religion and Revolution: Options in 1776," Pennsylvania *Mennonite Heritage* (July, 1978), 8. In 1781 a Loyalist named Hugh Kelly avoided a treason trial in Maryland by hiding in the woods. During this time he grew a long beard and was able to escape, donning Dunker garb and convincing the authorities he was a simple German Baptist.

Minutes of the Annual Meetings of the Old German Baptist Brethren from 1778 to 1955 (Winona Lake, IN, 1981). The Brethren passed numerous guidelines on personal appearance: 1804—beards are made mandatory for all elders; 1847—members are admonished to not be inconsistent in wearing plain clothing for meeting and fashionable clothing for other gatherings; 1848—it is required that all sisters wear a covering on their heads; 1856—the decision was made, "The plain cap, as worn by our dear aged sisters, is a covering as required by the scriptures according to Paul"; 1877—the standing collar on the coat was established as the old order as recognized by the Brethren. (See also note 23 for Brethren references.)

28. *Minutes of the General Conferences of Brethren in Christ, 1871-1904* (Harrisburg, PA, 1904). At the 1872 conference it was asked, "Is it according to gospel to have one given form of dress? Answer: It should not be in fashion with the world." In 1880 it was "decided to retain the plain apparel throughout the church."

29. *George Fox, A Collection of Many Select and Christian Epistles, Letters, and Testimonies* (London 1698), 249-250. George Fox, founder of the Society of Friends, wrote, "Friends, keep out of the vain fashions of the world; let not your eyes, and minds, and spirits run after every fashion (in attire) of the nations; for that will lead you from the solid life into unity with that spirit that leads to follow the fashions of the nations, after every fashion of apparel that gets up: but mind that which is sober and modest, and keep to your plain fashions, that you may judge the World, . . . "

William C. Braithwaite, *The Second Period of Quakerism* (London, 1919), 513. In 1698 a Quaker directive from Scotland spells out clothing standards which were fairly normative for conservative Friends for the next two hundred years. Men's coats were to be buttoned to the top so as not to make a show of their cravats. Extra buttons and outside pockets were prohibited. Hats were to have broad hat bands and were not to be cocked up on the sides. The women were to wear a plain coif (cap), a plain hood, and plain bands (cape).

Amelia Gummere, *The Quaker: A Study in Costume* (Philadelphia, 1901), 9. In 1732 a Jesuit priest came from Baltimore to Philadelphia and decided to adopt the Quaker habit to be inoffensive.

William T. Parsons, "The Bloody Election of 1742," *Pennsylvania History*, XXXIV, 3 (July, 1969), 298. A group of rowdy sailors, presumably hired to prevent Quakers from taking part in an election, thus identified their victims: "They are the men we want, men with broad hats and no pockets."

Edward Hocker, "Montgomery County History," *Bulletin of the Montgomery County Historical Society* (Fall, 1959), 64-65. In 1833 the Haverford (Quaker) College catalog called teachers to be examples of "plainness of dress and address and as for students, "that this body-coat, round jacket and waistcoat shall be single-breasted and without lapels or falling collars, and where any of these are figured they shall be of a pattern consistent with the plainness required in other parts of the dress—the students to wear hats, caps being excluded."

Logan Pearsall Smith, *Philadelphia Quaker, The Letters of Hannah Whitall Smith* (New York, 1950), 36. In 1877 a Quaker girl tells of a visiting minister who was refused a seat with the ministers in some meetings near Philadelphia because of the turndown collar on his coat.

Chapter 11—Women's Clothing

1. Alma Oakes and Margot Hamilton Hill, *Rural Costume* (London, 1970), 80.
2. Beverly Gordon, *Shaker Textile Arts* (Hanover, NH, 1980), 156.
3. Oakes, *Rural Costume*, 39.
4. Eli D. Wenger, *The Weaverland Mennonites* (Gordonville, PA, 1968), 88.
5. Claudia Kidwell, "Short Gowns," Dress (1978), 30-65.
6. Frederick Lewis Allen, *Only Yesterday* (New York, 1931), 73-101.
7. See Redmond Coyngham, Chapter 3, Note 23.
8. Oakes, *Rural Costume*, 99.
9. Anne Buck, *Dress in Eighteenth Century England* (New York, 19), 127.
10. Linda Grant DePauw and Conover Hunt, *Remember the Ladies* (New York, 1976), 114; Elizabeth McClellan, *Historic Dress in America 1607-1870* (New York, 1977), 225; Anonymous, *The Friends' Meeting House* (Philadelphia, 1904), plate facing page 100. The old drawing is entitled, 'The Bee-hive bonnet," but it more closely resembles a wagon bonnet.
11. James Lauer, *A Concise History of Costume* (London, 1969), 168, 172; Herman Williams, *Mirror to the American Past* (Greenwich, CT, 1973), plate 117 shows an 1840 painting by William Henry Burr, which clearly illustrates plain bonnets worn by working women and a fashionable bonnet worn by a wealthy woman. Most of the women also wear shawls.
12. Geoffrey Squire, *Dress and Society 1560-1970* (New York, 1974), 159; Alison Gernsheim, *Victorian and Edwardian Fashion, A Photographic Survey* (New York, 1963), 25-26; C. Willet Cunnington and Phillis Cunnington, *Handbook of English Costume in the Nineteenth Century* (Boston, 1970), 16. "The peculiar spirit of the Victorian era, distinguishing it from all others, was its moral sensibility."
13. See Chapter 3, Note 13.
14. Ira D. Landis, "Christian Women's Head Covering," *Mennonite Research Journal*, 8 (January, 1972), 6.
15. Edwin Deming Andrews, *The People Called Shakers* (New York, 1953), 25.

Chapter 12—Men's Clothing

1. *Johannes Kesslers Sabatta.* See Chapter 3, Note 3.
2. Isaiah 50:6.
3. Leviticus 19:27.
4. Penelope Byrde, *The Male Image* (London, 1979), 76.
5. Millia Davenport, *The Book of Costume* (New York, 1948), 160.
6. C. Willet Cunnington and Phillis Cunnington, *Handbook of English Costume in the 18th Century* (London, 1957), 58, 197; Byrde, *The Male Image*, 82; Anne Buck, *Dress in 18th Century England* (New York, 1979), 56.
7. See Morgan Edwards, Chapter 3, Note 23, and William Parsons, Chapter 3, Note 29.
8. Cunnington, *Handbook of English Costume in the Eighteenth Century*, passim; Aileen Ribeiro, *A Visual History of Costume, The Eighteenth Century* (London and New York, 1983),

passim.

9. C. Willet Cunnington and Phillis Cunnington, *Handbook of English Costume in the Nineteenth Century* (Boston, 1970), passism; Byrde, *The Male Image,* passison; Elizabeth McClellan, *Historic Dress in America 1607-1870* (New York, 1977), passism.

10. *1877 Annual Meeting of the German Baptist Brethren, Full Report,* article 9.

11. Eva F. Sprunger, *The First Hundred Years* (Berne, IN, 1938), 19, 25-26.

12. Samuel Floyd Pannabecker, *Faith in Ferment* (Newton, KS, 1968), 148.

13. *Quaker Biographies Series II,* I-V (Philadelphia, n.d.), passim; Melvin Gingerich, *Mennonite Attire through Four Centuries* (Breinigsville, PA, 1970), 12, 49, 51, 69, 99; John L. Ruth, *Maintaining the Right Fellowship* (Scottdale, PA, 1984), 75; Richard L. Hostetter, "Descendants of Immigrant Jacob Hostetter," *Pennsylvania Mennonite Heritage,* 6 (April, 1983), 23; A. J. Fretz, *A Genealogical Record of The Descendants of Christian and Hans Meyer* (Harleysville, PA, 1896), plate facing page 134 (or 168, in some copies, paging varies); *The Reesor Family in Canada* (1980), 75.

14. Eli D. Wenger, *The Weaverland Mennonites* (Gordonville, PA, 1968), 89.

15. *Cunnington, Handbook of English Costume in the Nineteenth Century,* 160, 199.

16. See chapter 3, Note 14.

17. John C. Wenger, "The Alms Book of the Franconia Mennonite Church, 1767-1936," *Mennonite Quarterly Review* (July, 1936), 171.

18. Melvin Gingerich, *Mennonite Attire through Four Centuries* (Breinigsville, PA, 1970), 56.

19. *Cunnington, Handbook of English Costume in the Eighteenth Century,* 214.

20. Ellen Gehret, *Rural Pennsylvania Clothing* (York, 1976), 154.

21. *Cunnington, Handbook of English Costume in the Eighteenth Century,* 232; Davenport, *The Book of Costume,* 798.

22. C. Henry Smith, *Smith's Story of The Mennonites* (Newton, Kansas, 1981), 164.

Chapter 13—Dress in Detail

1. Several Lancaster daughter settlements observe the same dress practices.

2. Until about age 13 girls wear a cap only for church and a few other formal occasions.

3. A dress buttoning up the back with a gathered skirt is worn until age 11 or 12.

4. A girl wears a white cap to church until age 13, then changes to a black cap (except for some districts in the eastern part of the community where girls do not wear black caps). After about age 30, single women wear white caps at church.

5. For non-church, dress-up occasions, from ages 8 to 11, girls wear black capes.

6. Occasionally some single girls wear black capes.

7. A cape matching the dress is worn by most married and single women until about age 40, after which a black cape is worn. Ministers' wives always wear black capes.

8. School-age girls wear either black or white caps for everyday. Teenage girls wear white caps except for church. This is true for most places where it is indicated on the chart that white or black caps are worn by singles.

9. Everyday aprons are sometimes tied in back.

10. A one-piece underdress is worn beneath the two-piece outer dress in cold weather. For everyday wear a sleeveless bodice is sometimes worn which exposes the long sleeves of the white shirt which is worn as an undergarment.

11. A cape and apron are worn under the pinafore apron.

12. Straw, flat hats with black ribbon trimming are now very infrequently worn, usually just for walking to church or working outside.

13. The clothing customs of Geauga County, Ohio, are nearly identical to those of Holmes County, Ohio. The Andy Weaver group in Holmes County is slightly more conservative than the largest group. The New Order group is slightly less conservative, except the cape is worn more frequently, and unmarried men have longer beards.

14. Also located in two other settlements in Ohio and in Tennessee, Ontario, New York, Minnesota, and Michigan. The Troyer Amish are nearly identical. They are found in Ohio, New York, Ontario, Pennsylvania, and Michigan.

15. Girls wear black caps daily until baptism, after which they wear black only for

Old Order Mennonites, Ontario

church and white otherwise.

16. The Amish in neighboring Elkhart County are much the same as those in LaGrange County. One difference is that the women in Elkhart wear the straight cape. The community at Nappanee, Indiana, is also much like LaGrange in most respects.

17. A number of midwestern communities are similar if not identical to Buchanan. These include Clark, Missouri; McIntire, Iowa; Utice, Minnesota; and Wilton, Wisconsin. The settlements at Bowling Green, Missouri; Cashton, Wisconsin; and Mt. Elgin, Ontario, are also similar.

18. The bonnet brim is to extend to a point level with the end of the nose.

19. There are two distinct groups in Adams County, and standards may vary within the same group.

20. At about age 2 a boy gets a plain-crown, felt hat. At about age 10 this is exchanged for a telescoped hat. That style is worn until about age 40, when a man returns to a plain-crown hat. All ministers wear plain-crown hats with 4" brims.

21. Lancaster young men get a frock coat at age 16 whether they are baptized or not. After this a sack coat is not worn.

22. Formerly most young men wore telescoped-crown hats. This custom is less common currently.

23. Felt hats do not have the usual edge binding.

24. Some small boys do wear suspenders.

25. Hip pockets are allowed on pants.

26. There are two distinct groups in Adams County with slightly differing dress customs.

27. Ministers wear dark blue shirts to church.

28. The Wisler Mennonites of Indiana and Ohio and the Markahm-Waterloo Mennonites of Ontario arc very similar to the Hornings.

29. In most Old Order Mennonite groups white covering strings are worn during early marriage, then a change to black strings is made. Many younger Horning women wear covering strings only for church. Horning girls wear their hair in braids until between ages 9 and 12, then they change to wearing a ponytail. Many begin wearing their hair up with a covering by age 14 or 15.

30. The Reidenbach or "Thirty-Fiver" Mennonites of Lancaster County and the Old Order Mennonites of Indiana are very similar to the Wengers.

31. The head covering is only worn for church from age 2 to 16. Babies have pale pink or green tie strings. The hair is worn in braids until age 13, then it is worn in a bun.

32. Dark blue or brown bonnets are worn to church until age 13, then a black bonnet is worn. Girls wear sunbonnets of fine prints (sometimes with a straw brim) to school in warm weather and soft bonnet-like capes in cold weather.

33. Shawls have been worn more frequently by girls until bicycle-riding became acceptable.

34. There are two groups of Old Order Mennonites in Virginia, both very similar in dress.

35. Girls wear bonnets in church rather than coverings before they are baptized.

36. This group has become increasingly more conservative in this respect in the 1980s.

37. The David Martin Mennonites of this community are very similar to the Woolwich group, except men's hat brims are wider; boys wear darker-colored neckties until marriage, after which they do not wear them at all; at about age 32 men begin wearing plain suits with dark blue shirts, in church young men wear light blue shirts; women wear darker-colored dresses, have lace on the edge of their coverings (an old custom), wear small, hard-crown, "Victoria" bonnets year-round; girls wear sunbonnets made of print material and wear winter caps with a one-piece crown.

38. No head covering is worn until age 14, and from then until marriage it is worn only at church.

39. The winter bonnet is called a Queen Anne or Victoria bonnet. Single women have a bow on top of these bonnets. School girls wear large, blue, sunbonnets in summer and close-fitting heavy caps with a neck curtain and three-piece crown in winter.

40. Most men wear a billed, "box cap" with ear flaps in winter.

41. A frock coat with turnover collar and lapels is worn for baptism and marriage. Young men wear white shirts and older men light blue shirts at church.

42. There are several related groups, most with very similar dress practices. The Hoover Mennonites (of PA, KY, TN, ON) are exceptional in that the men wear beards.

43. Stauffer girls always wear their hair up. The head covering is only worn to church by younger, unbaptized girls. Some teenage girls wear the traditional covering or a more modern style covering for daily wear. Covering strings are various colors, often blue, until about age 10.

44. Girls wear various colored bonnets until age 16. Blue is preferred by older girls, who then change to a black bonnet.

45. The coat is to have the "shad belly" cut. All work coats must have a standing collar or no collar.

46. The members of the Independent Brethren Church of Pennsylvania are very similar to the conservative element in the Church of the Brethren from which they withdrew in 1972. Many men wear beards.

47. The Conservative German Baptist Church withdrew from the Dunkard Brethren in 1931. This church requires the beard and frock coat for ministers, and suspenders and high shoes for all men. Women wear large coverings with tied strings, rectangular-style cape dresses, black stockings, and small, chin-strap bonnets.

The Bible Brethren of Pennsylvania (divided from the Church of the Brethren in 1948) are similar to Dunkard Brethren, except ministers are required to wear the beard and frock coat and all women wear the cape dress and black stockings. The Christ's Ambassadors came from the Bible Brethren in 1974. They do not have definite dress standards but are similar to the Dunkard Brethren. Many women wear opaque white head coverings.

The Conservative Brethren of Virginia are also similar to the Dunkard Brethren except all women wear the cape dress and dark stockings. Covering strings are not required and wristwatches (with dark bands) are allowed.

48. The Old Brethren Church (Salida Brethren) is very similar to the Old German Brethren except that men may wear a mustache with the beard and women are not required to wear the apron. Christ's Assembly is also very similar except there are no definite rules on dress. Many women wear large opaque white head coverings with a neck curtain. Men may wear a mustache with the beard.

49. Three separate fellowships, all quite similar.

Readings and Sources

Life and History of the Plain People

Andrews, Edward Deming. *The People Called Shakers.* New York: Dover, 1953.

Cragg, Perry. *The Amish, A Photographic Album.* Cleveland: Dillon/Liederbach, 1971.

Cronk, Sandra. "Gelassenheit: The Rites of Redemptive Process in Old Order Amish and Old Order Mennonite Communities." *Mennonite Quarterly Review,* 55, No. 1 (January, 1981), 5-44.

Durnbaugh, Donald, ed. *The Brethren Encyclopedia.* Oak Brook, Illinois and Philadelphia: The Brethren Encyclopedia, 1983.

Durnbaugh, Donald. *Meet the Brethren.* Elgin, Illinois: The Brethren Press, 1984.

Dyck, Cornelius J., ed. *An Introduction to Mennonite History.* Scottdale, Pennsylvania: Herald Press, 1967.

Epp, Frank H. *Mennonites in Canada 1786-1920.* Toronto: Macmillan, 1974.

____. *Mennonites in Canada 1920-1940.* Scottdale, Pennsylvania: Herald Press, 1982.

Denlinger, A. Martha. *Real People.* Scottdale, Pennsylvania: Herald Press, 1975.

Denlinger, Steven L. *Glimpses Past.* Lancaster, Pennsylvania: Historical Society, 1985.

Fisher, Sara E. and Stahl, Rachel K. *The Amish School.* Intercourse, Pennsylvania: Good Books, 1986.

Gingerich, Orland. *The Amish of Canada.* Scottdale, Pennsylvania: Herald Press, 1972.

Good, Merle. *Who Are the Amish?* Intercourse, Pennsylvania: Good Books, 1985.

Good, Merle and Phyllis. *Twenty Most Asked Questions About the Amish and Mennonites.* Intercourse, Pennsylvania: Good Books, 1979.

Gross, Paul S. *The Hutterite Way.* Saskatoon, Saskatchewan: Freeman, 1965.

Hiebert, Clarence. *The Holdeman People.* South Pasadena, California: William Carey Library, 1973.

Horst, Isaac R. *Separate and Peculiar.* Mt. Forest, Ontario: Isaac R. Horst, 1979.

Hostetler, John A. *Amish Society.* Baltimore, Maryland: Johns Hopkins University Press, 1980.

Hostetler, John A. *Hutterite Society.* Baltimore, Maryland: Johns Hopkins University Press, 1974.

Hunsberger, David L. *People Apart.* St. Jacobs, Ontario: Sand Hills Books, 1977.

Klopfenstein, Perry A. *Marching to Zion, A History of the Apostolic Christian Church in America 1847-1982.* Ft. Scott, Kansas: Sekan Printing, 1984.

Kraybill, Paul N. *Mennonite World Handbook.* Lombard, Illinois: Mennonite World Conference, 1978.

Mennonite Encyclopedia, The. Scottdale, Pennsylvania: Herald Press, 1959.

Miller, Levi. *Our People, The Amish and Mennonites of Ohio.* Scottdale, Pennsylvania: Herald Press, 1983.

Pearson, Elmer R., and Neal, Julia. *The Shaker Image.* Boston: New York Graphic Society, 1974.

Pellman, Kenneth and Rachel. *The World of Amish Quilts.* Intercourse, Pennsylvania: Good Books, 1984.

Redekop, Calvin. *The Old Colony Mennonites.* Baltimore, Maryland: Johns Hopkins University Press, 1969.s

Rice, Charles S. and Shenk, John B. *Meet the Amish.* New Brunswick, New Jersey: Rutgers University Press, 1947.

Russel, Elbert. *The History of Quakerism.* New York: Macmillan, 1942.

Ruth, John L. *A Quiet and Peaceable Life.* Intercourse, Pennsylvania: Good Books, 1979, 1985.

Sawatzky, Harry Leonard. *They Sought a Country,* Berkeley, California: University of California Press, 1971.

Scott, Stephen. "The Old Order River Brethren," *Pennsylvania Mennonite Heritage,* I, No. 3 (July, 1978), 13-22.

Smith, Elmer, *Meet the Mennonites.* Witmer, Pennsylvania: Applied Arts, 1961.

Wenger, Eli D. *The Weaverland Mennonites.* Gordonville, Pennsylvania: 1968.

Wittlinger, Carlton O. *Quest for Piety and Obedience.* Nappanee, Indiana: Evangel Press, 1978.

Zug, Joan Liffring and John Zug. *The Amanas Yesterday.* Amana, Iowa: The Amana Society, 1975.

Plain Clothing

Berky, Andrew S. "Buckskin or Sackcloth? A Glance at the Clothing Once Worn by Schwenkfelders in Pennsylvania," *Pennsylvania Folklife* (Spring, 1958), 50-52.

Gingerich, Melvin. *Mennonite Attire Through Four Centuries.* Breinigsville, Pennsylvania: The Pennsylvania German Society, 1970.

Gordon, Beverly. *Shaker Textile Arts.* Hanover, New Hampshire: University Press of New England, 1980.

Gummere, Amelia Mott. *The Quaker, A Study in Costume.* New York/London: Benjamin Blom, 1968.

Hershey, Mary Jane. "A Study of the Dress of the (Old) Mennonites of the Franconia Conference 1700-1953," *Pennsylvania Folklife* (Spring, 1958), 24-47.

Hostetler, John A. "Amish Costume: Its European Origins," *The American German Review,* 22 (August/September, 1956), 11-14.

Kendall, Joan. "The Development of a Distinctive Form of Quaker Dress," *Costume,* 19 (1985), 58-74.

Milbern, Gwendolyn, *Shaker Clothing.* Lebanon, Ohio: Warren County Historical Society, n.d.

Rupel, Esther Fern. *An Investigation of the Origin, Significance, and Demise of the Prescribed Dress Worn by Members of the Church of the Brethren.* Ann Arbor, Michigan: University Micro Films, 1980.

Shiess, Kate. "The Costume of a Plain People," *Threads* (June/July, 1986), 65-69.

Yoder, Don. "Sectarian Costume Research in the United States," *Forms Upon the Frontier.* Logan, Utah: Utah University Press, 1969.

Religious Basis for Plain Clothing

Annable, E. B. *Light on the Wedding Ring*. Harrisonburg, Virginia: Sword and Trumpet, n.d.

Anonymous. *The Bible on Immodest Apparel*. Hesston, Kansas: Free Tract and Bible Society, Church of God in Christ Mennonite, n.d.

Anonymous. *Plain Dressing*. General Mission Board, Dunkard Brethren Church, n.d.

Bontrager, Levi. *Why Should Men Wear Beards?* Hesston, Kansas: Free Tract and Bible Society, Church of God in Christ, Mennonite, n.d.

Brunk, George R. *The Bible on Dress*. Crockett, Kentucky: Rod and Staff Publisher, n.d

Crist, D. A. *The Doctrine of the Prayer Veil*. General Mission Board, Dunkard Brethren Church, n.d.

Hartzler, Lloyd. *Personal Appearance in the Light of God's Word*. Harrisonburg, Virginia: Christian Light Publications, n.d

Horsch, John. *Worldly Conformity in Dress*. Scottdale, Pennsylvania: Mennonite Publishing House, 1926.

Horst, Melvin G. *Distinctive Attire for Christians*. Crockett, Kentucky: Rod and Staff Publishers, n.d.

McGrath, William R. *Separation Throughout Church History*. Seymour, Missouri: Edgewood Press, 1966.

____. *Why I Wear a Beard*. Hayesville, North Carolina, n.d.

____. *Why We Wear Plain Clothes*. Mission Home, Virginia, n.d.

____. *Christlicher Ordnung or Christian Discipline*. Aylmer, Ontario: Pathway Publishing House, 1966.

Martin, Harold S. *The Bible Doctrine of Non-Conformity*. Hanover, Pennsylvania: Bible Helps, n.d.

____. *The Scriptural Head Veiling*. Hanover, Pennsylvania: Bible Helps, n.d.

Mennonite General Conference. *Dress, A Brief Treatise*. Aylmer, Ontario: Pathway Publishing House, 1967 (reprinted from 1921 original).

Riehl, Aquilla. *The Christian Woman's Head Covering*. Crockett, Kentucky: Rod and Staff Publishers, n.d.

Stauffer, John L. *Why Should Christians Wear a Distinctive Attire?* Crockett, Kentucky: Rod and Staff Publishers, n.d.

Wenger, John C. *Christianity and Dress*. Scottdale, Pennsylvania: Herald Press, 1944.

____. *Historical and Biblical Position of the Mennonite Church on Attire*. Scottdale, Pennsylvania: Herald Press, 1944.

____. *The Prayer Veil, In Scripture and History*. Scottdale, Pennsylvania: Herald Press, 1964.

Wenger, Wayne J. *The Wearing or the Non-Wearing of the Tie*. Crockett, Kentucky: Rod and Staff Publishers, n.d.

Costume History

Allen, Frederick Lewis. *Only Yesterday.* New York: Harper and Brothers, 1931.

Buck, Anne. *Dress in Eighteenth Century England.* New York: Holmes and Meier, 1979.

Byrde, Penelope. *The Male Image.* London: B. T. Batsford, Ltd., 1979.

Cunnington, C. Willet and Phillis. *Handbook of English Costume in the Sixteenth Century.* Boston: Plays, Inc., 1970.

____. *Handbook of English Costume in the Seventeenth Century.* Boston: Plays, Inc., 1973.

____. *Handbook of English Costume in the Eighteenth Century.* Boston: Plays, Inc., 1972.

____. *Handbook of English Costume in the Nineteenth Century.* Boston: Plays, Inc., 1970.

Cunnington, Phillis. *Costume of Household Servants.* New York: Barnes and Noble, 1974.

Cunnington, Phillis and Lucas, Catherine. *Charity Costumes.* New York: Barnes and Noble, 1978.

____. *Occupational Costume in England.* London: Adam and Charles Black, 1967.

Davenport, Millia. *The Book of Costume.* New York: Crown, 1948.

Fennelly, Catherine. *The Garb of Country New Englanders 1790-1840.* Sturbridge, Massachusetts: Old Sturbridge Village, 1966.

Gehret, Ellen J. *Rural Pennsylvania Clothing.* York, Pennsylvania: Liberty Cap, 1976.

Gernsheim, Alison. *Victorian and Edwardian Fashion, A Photographic Survey.* New York: 1963.

Kidwell, Claudia. "Short Gowns," *Dress,* 4 (1978), 30-65.

____. *Suiting Everyone.* Washington, D.C.: Smithsonian Institution Press, 1974.

Lauer, James. *A Concise History of Costume.* London: Thames and Hudson, 1964.

Lurie, Alison. *The Language of Clothes.* New York: Random House, 1981.

McClellan, Elizabeth. *Historic Dress in America 1607-1870.* New York, Arno Press, 1977.

Oakes, Alma, and Hill, Margot Hamilton. *Rural Costume.* London: B. T. Batsford, Ltd., 1970.

Rebeiro, Aileen. *A Visual History of Costume, the Eighteenth Century.* London and New York: Drama, 1983.

Snowden, James. *The Folk Dress of Europe.* New York: Mayflower, 1979.

Squire, Geoffrey. *Dress and Society 1560-1970.* New York: Viking, 1974.

Vincent, John Martin. *Costume and Conduct in the Laws of Bazel, Bern and Zurich, 1370-1800.* Baltimore, Maryland: Johns Hopkins Press, 1935.

Index

About the Author

Stephen E. Scott grew up between Dayton and Xenia, Ohio, on the outskirts of the largest community of Old German Baptist Brethren. In his youth, Steve was a member of a Missionary Baptist Church but was deeply impressed by the simple, godly life of the plain people. He began visiting with various plain groups in Ohio and eventually worked, worshiped, and lived with them. In 1969 Steve moved to Lancaster County, Pennsylvania. Here he joined the Old Order River Brethren, a group of conservative plain people.

Steve studied at Cedarville (Ohio) College and has been a teacher.

He is the author of these books: *Plain Buggies; Amish, Mennonite, and Brethren Horse-Drawn Transportation; The Amish Wedding and Other Special Occasions of the Old Order Communities;* and *An Introduction to Old Order and Conservative Mennonite Groups.* He is co-author with Kenneth Pellman of *Living Without Electricity?*

Steve is married to Harriet Sauder. They are the parents of three children, Andrew, Hannah, and Catharine, and live near Columbia, PA.